THE SONGWRITER'S SURVIVAL GUIDE TO SUCCESS

Dude McLean

EDITED BY RONNY SCHIFF

HAL•LEONARD®

HAL LEONARD BOOKS
An Imprint of Hal Leonard Corporation
New York

Published in 2010 by Hal Leonard Books
An Imprint of Hal Leonard Corporation
7777 West Bluemound Road
Milwaukee, WI 53213

Trade Book Division Editorial Offices
19 West 21st Street, New York, NY 10010

www.halleonard.com

Book design by Kristina Rolander
Front cover design by Michael Kellner

Library of Congress Cataloging-in-Publication Data

McLean, Dude.
 The songwriter's survival guide to success : how to pitch your songs / Dude McLean.
    p. cm.
 ISBN 978-1-4234-8885-9
 1. Popular music--Writing and publishing--Vocational guidance. I. Title.
 ML3795M356 2010
 782.42164023--dc22

                          2010021530

Printed in the United States of America

Contents

The Brill Building—music publishing history was made here...

Introduction

There is an art to getting your songs seen by the decision makers. It is a long and twisting road, and the learning curve seems to go on and on. That's because, like all businesses, the music business is in a constant state of flux.

In the music business it's not always easy to get real and accurate inside information. The information you find packed into this book is very real, very serious, and there are no punches pulled. Each and every page is a lesson on how to achieve your goal.

This book is about your career as a songwriter, and how to handle that career. It's jammed with information for you—you as a songwriter. I'm assuming that you already know certain facts about being a songwriter. I am not going to teach you how to write a song or about contracts and other information related to the music business; plenty of other fine books already cover those areas (see the Recommended Reading List at the back of this book). Instead, this is about how to get your songs in front of the real decision makers.

I'll show you how to operate and move your songs every day.
You will find some unique ways to connect with those producers, publishers, managers, artists, A&R people, and all the VIPs you need to contact.

If you really want a career as a songwriter, then all you need to do is get out of that chair and apply what is revealed in this book.

Build It, and They Will Come

By building your career step-by-step and song-by-song, "they" will come knocking on your door. Every tip and trick in this book is a brick that will help you build your own house of songs. All you have to do is stack those bricks using strong mortar to hold it all together. Your songs are the mortar.

I have packed all I know about getting songs in front of the right people into this book, and if you are serious about your songwriting career, you now need to motivate and apply yourself. You are holding a ticket to ride. Jump on; it's gonna be a roller coaster.

Just to Pump You Up

Think about it. Being a songwriter ... what a great way to make a living, a life, and a career.

A Few Comments

Before you plunge headlong into this work, here are a few observations: Clearly, I realize that some methods disclosed may not always be politically correct. Use those steps or variations at your discretion.

- ▸ Working hard does not automatically guarantee success, but working hard and working smart ups those chances.

- ▸ It is all about your end product—the song. Is it any good? Did you produce a real piece of material?

- ▸ I will help you determine whether you have the song and how to get it in front of the right people.

Now let's go for it!

Is Your Song Competitive?

I'm a Songwriter ... Now What?

You want to be a songwriter. Or, you are already a songwriter. Great! Now what? You have a box full of songs and need somewhere to go.

Perhaps you have tried to get your songs heard and have "pitched" your songs a few times. That's a start. You might even be among those writers who have had some songs recorded, and so now you feel that you are on your way.

So let's get to it: this is your career!

About Your Song, Your Creation, Your "Baby"

You need to develop a tough skin. Here are some facts. First, learn the realities of the business. Ask yourself these questions: Why will the artist want to record my song? What makes my song so different? Why record my song instead of someone else's? Why is my song better than the songs the artist is writing?

You don't need to suck up and tell the producer or artist or publisher that you wrote the song just for them. Fact: they don't really care. When the people you want to impress with your song "hear" that great piece of material that they must record, they don't need any more hype (read, begging, from you).

CHAPTER 2

Know the Songs That Came Before You

There is an area of the music business that drives me nuts and that I find appalling: the ignorance of some songwriters, producers, artists, and publishers about the styles of music. Know the history; listen to old songs. Know the background of your craft. Don't let your ego fool you into believing that you are the only one who ever thought of a particular idea. Immerse yourself in the hits and standards. Listen to the original recordings. Who were the writers of any given era, and what influence did they have on modern music? Know the songs that came before you. Before Elvis. Before the Beatles. Before Bruce, Madonna, Kurt, and Michael.

There are songs that were initially huge hits in the 1920s, and then again in every decade after that. "Smoke Gets in Your Eyes" was in the 1933 Broadway show called *Roberta*, on the charts in 1934, in the film adaptation of the Broadway show in 1935, on various records in 1946, and then twice in the 1950s—all chart hits. The song was also in the 1973 movie *American Graffiti*, in the 2004 Golden Globe–winning film *Being Julia*, and on the 2009 Barbra Streisand album *Love Is the Answer*. Pink Martini does great covers of old songs, so did Michael Jackson, and so do Michael Bublé and Queen Latifah. Songwriting and pitching songs didn't start when you did!

I have a personal aversion to plugging or working with a song title that has been used before, and especially if the title was a standard. It leads to confusion, and your royalties could possibly go to the other songs of that title. You can't copyright a title, as you know (or should know). Come up with your own original title.

Think about it ... songs are ephemeral: you can't touch them and you can't see them, but you do feel and hear them. They will haunt you, and they pop up in the strangest places and at the most unexpected times. They can change your life and lead you in other directions. Songs often provide a psychic connection between people. Songs can be powerful and tender, drama filled, and happy or sad. They can move you to laughter and tears, and their names should be unique.

To my mind, "standards" are those that have stood the test of time. Look at the covers of Tom Waits's and Leonard Cohen's songs.

Musical tastes change; artists come and go, they fade into oblivion, and their work may be forgotten. But is it forgotten? The test is when you play a song for a person who has never heard of a particular artist (or song) but who is into "songs," and they are stunned. "My god, that song is 50 years old and they were writing like that?" The level of sophistication in lyrics or music certainly is nothing new. Go back sixty, seventy, or eighty years and more, and you can compile long lists of fabulous songs. Conversely, the list of so-so songs, terrible songs, and so on, is so long that the sheet music would wrap around the world—more than once.

The point is that you as an artist, a songwriter, a song plugger or producer, or a music publisher can learn much from these past masters. Painters study all the old masters, as do sculptors and architects. So why should songwriters be any different? This is an area waiting to be mined and discovered by you. It will make you stronger and better at your craft. Songs are interpreted by singers, and they too should study the "old master" songwriters. (The same goes for producers and the music publishers.)

> ‣ I strongly urge that you study the standards and the masters of songwriting.
>
> ‣ Know the artists, writers, and producers (producers didn't get liner-note credits until the late '50s).
>
> ‣ In today's world, it is easy to hear the old recordings on iTunes and other MP3-download sites.

One point about these songwriters: like painters, not every one of their works is a masterstroke. Know those songs that are the diamonds finely cut with a brilliance that defies time, and that are always fresh and untarnished. "Evergreen" is a word used by music publishers to describe classic songs. You also have to consider the era into which many of these songs fit. Some classics are silly songs, but that was a part of the times. Keep that in mind.

CHAPTER 3

Kennel Blindness

A Big Part of Knowing Your Song

The term *kennel blind* is used in dog-breeding circles and by those who show dogs. It's a statement you hear about a dog breeder who continues to show a dog in spite of its obvious faults and the remarks of judges that the dog will never win a competition—the standard just won't allow it. Unfortunately, there is no such standard in the writing of songs because songwriting is far more subjective. The point is this: recognize the faults in your song. Also recognize its good points. If the good outweighs the bad by a strong margin, then you are ahead of the game. If you fail to observe the major flaws in your song, then you are being "kennel blind."

One of the challenges for the writer is to recognize if his or her song is a gem or just another stone. Sometimes the writer is the last person to know. Recognizing originality is not as easy as one might think. Just because a song is unusual or odd, it does not an original song make. It is in your job description to find a way to say "I love you" in a brand-new way that rolls off the tongue like sugar. It is also your job to find the right words in the language puzzle and combine them in a totally unique way. And it's your job to put these words together in a song that will express the idea "come into my life," "get out of my life," or "I love you so much I could move mountains."

If you study the masters of songwriting, it becomes an influential lesson about what songs can be and how they are written, and you will find the "art." When you write an original line about loving someone, it may feel uncomfortable to you because it's not your usual familiar sentiment. However, it should work and flow and be easy to say. Live with it for a while. Sometimes, changing just one word in a line makes it totally unique.

Try this trick: You have a verse of four lines. Take away the first line and now read your verse; does it still make sense? If your answer is "yes," ask yourself if you really need the first line. If your answer is "no," then you need the first line.

What I am getting at here is to work for your own voice in writing songs; say it your way, not the way all the other writers have, or the way that everyone's already heard before.

Kennel blindness occurs when you have worked hard on a song, played it over and over again—until you become convinced this is it. You overlook the flaws in the verse or that clumsy chord change, or you settle for a melody that doesn't fit the words well.

Listen to the Feedback and Fix Your Song

Feedback from friends is often positive. That's good and it helps out your ego a lot. The public in many cases is easy to please, but the professionals in the music business are much harder to please.

This is when real feedback comes into play: if you have the ear of a producer or a publisher and they have the time to talk to you about your creation, pay attention. Take the negative to heart, and turn it around. They may be right. If the publisher says to you that this section and that line do not work, ask them why not. Even if you do not agree with them, try the suggested changes. You have everything to gain.

On the other hand, if you choose to ignore what has been said, pitch your song to others anyway, and then get turned down, try to find out what they didn't like about your song. That is the hard part. Many times publishers will not be able to pinpoint the problem. Some professionals cannot articulate why they do not like a song, other than it just doesn't "work" for them.

Could it be the same problem the first publisher or producer pointed out to you? Could it be they were right? Could it be that the song does lose its focus and the melody doesn't fit? If you keep pitching the song and rejects keep happening, perhaps you have kennel blindness. Now is the time to be a pro and sit down, do a rewrite, and make it work.

Recognize which words are hard to sing and consider using a different word that may change the whole direction of the song. That's okay.

Try not to fool yourself into overlooking a part that doesn't flow, is unclear, or loses focus. If you think "they" won't notice, you are wrong.

This is a difficult perspective to attain, and it comes only with experience and being willing to listen and take advice when it is given. Similarly, knowing a song is just fine as it is comes with experience. Most hit songs were pitched many times before they were recorded.

For me, rule number 1 for a song is that you have to make the listener give a damn and hook the listener into the song. In other words, draw the listener into the world of the song. What you care about might not be important to the listener.

Consider the Subject Matter

You have a song; everything seems to work, but you cannot get it cut. Look at the subject matter.

If it is a story song, is it provocative? Does it grab the listener to the point that they want hear it all the way through? Are the emotions universal? Can people who have never been there relate and put themselves in that spot in their mind's eye? Is it too long? Even a true story doesn't work if you don't make the listener care.

If you have a love song, perhaps you are just saying the same thing the same old way. Maybe it's well crafted but lacks originality. If you are being redundant, repeating the same old lines, then you need to move in a different direction. If the song is well constructed but lacks the original touch, you have a case of kennel blindness.

Being objective about your own songs is difficult at best. Being honest with yourself is just as difficult. You need to be your own hard-nosed critic. Have you heard "I love you, sugarplum" said just like that in other songs? If so, then you need to work on that line and make it your own, or you will be lost in the land of kennel blindness.

CHAPTER 4

Opinions Are Like ...

How do you get opinions on the songs you are going to pitch—songs you are excited about? Is it something like this: "Hey, bro, this is S. Writer here. Man, I am excited by this song, can't wait to play it for you"?

And you play the song for your friends and relatives. Almost to a person, they will tell you it's great, wonderful, and a very good song! That's just super for your ego. We all need a shot in the arm once in a while. However, a reality check is in order. These people are your friends and relatives. First, they are easy to please. Second, they will not tell you to your face how they really feel about the song; they don't want to hurt your feelings or insult you. It is nice to sit around and play your songs for friends and family, but don't put too much stock in their opinions.

The next sets of ears that should hear your song are those of your songwriter friends. This group will have a mixed reaction of opinions and will give helpful hints on how to fix your song. Keep in mind, however, that many songwriters are some of the worst critics of someone else's songs. Why? Because the way you've expressed your message is not how they would have said it. It's not their "throw the pencil in the air" line. The next thing you know, you may be listening to their songs.

Some writers who hang out together develop a system for critiquing each other's songs, and for them that method seems to work (most of the time). Count yourself lucky if you are part of a group like that. The difference between this group and your friends and relatives is that these people are professionals, and that does help.

So if you are plugging and pitching songs, then you most likely know other pluggers and songwriters. You definitely want their opinions, but take it all with the proverbial grain of salt. Ask yourself, "Do I need opinions from other people, pros, writers, or anyone?" The uppermost thought in your mind should be, "This song is my vision, my feelings about it, my belief. Should it be subject to anybody's idea of why it works or why it doesn't?"

And remember that one of these kind critics might have a valid idea about whom to pitch the song to. Always keep in mind the real experience of whoever is giving advice about your material. Some people are born "song smart." They are the ones to seek out. Some folks are true mentors. Use what you can and dismiss the rest. One of the problems that has befallen our business is this: very seldom is it that just one person's decision determines that a song will be "the song." Often a song is picked by a committee: the producer, manager, artist, spouse, recording engineer, lawyer, barber, record company people, girl- or boyfriend, or even the limo driver.

HOT TIP

▸ None of these people will have any influence whatsoever in deciding whether this song will be cut by Miss Golden Pipes. Period.

▸ Do not fall into the trap of picking your songs by committee.

▸ This is a lonely business.

▸ You had best get used to it.

CHAPTER **5**

Noise-and-Nonsense and Casting

Songs You Think Are Your Competition

HOT TIP

- Do not compare your songs with any songs that an artist writes and sings.

- How many times have you heard a song by Miss Golden Pipes and you think to yourself, "My songs are better than that!"? You shouldn't torture yourself with those kinds of thoughts.

- Remember, an artist-written song is not your competition. Period.

- No matter how good or bad, brilliant, or noise-and-nonsense the songs are, they are recorded because the artist has a record deal.

Songs Written by Artists

With few exceptions, most songs written by artists would never stand on their own in a pile of songs all good enough to demand attention. In many cases, artist-written songs are wanting in professional quality, and that's being kind! So they don't count.

I'm not talking about the true singer-songwriters here. I'm talking about the kind of singer who decides, "Gee, I can write a song, too." In many cases, I think not.

Your real competition comes from songwriters who are the true professionals. Granted, some of those songs are recorded because of the reputation of the writer, and not because of the quality of the song. This proves my theory that most producers and artists may be clueless about what makes a great song and, more importantly, which song fits which artist. Opinions about any given song are subjective, but experience and a track record do help.

- Show me the entire catalogue of songs written by any pro writer who has been around a while, and I will bet you that in that catalogue will be anywhere from dozens to hundreds of songs that have never been recorded and never will be.

- The reason is that the songs are either just okay, not very good, or lousy to awful.

- Not all songs written are killer songs.

- For every 10 or 20 songs you write, you will be lucky if one is worth working with, pitching, or listening to ever again.

- So, beware of your own "noise and nonsense."

You need to pick and choose your songs carefully for whatever artist you are pitching. Don't pitch a song for which the artist has no range. A real "singer's song" is not for many artists. The reason is that most are not singers; they are stylists. They are limited in the kinds of material they can handle. Be smart about your songs and for whom they will work. Don't fool yourself into believing your song is for everybody. Believe me, it is not!

Pitching songs is an art form unto itself. Say you have 30 songs with which you are working. Make a list of those songs. Make a list of the producers and artists who are coming up. Write the song title beside each artist's name. Now play the song you have in mind. Do not play it in your mind, but rather play the demo out loud. Does it really fit that artist? Be brutal. Be honest. If you don't think the song fits, pass on the pitch. Wait until you have the perfect song for that artist. You'll be better off.

I can teach you craft...
...Ideas
...Tricks
Give you tools to use.
But...
I cannot teach you brilliance.
That's why you are the songwriter.

CHAPTER 6

Create a Niche Song

Novelty songs fill a niche. Sometimes you may not even know you are filling a niche. But the history of songwriting is filled with different and eccentric songs. When you say whether a song's a novelty song, or odd, or political, the distinction can become blurred. A perfect example can be seen in the song "Itsy Bitsy Teeny Weeny Yellow Polka Dot Bikini." It went from being a hit as a novelty, to movies and TV, and on to commercials that just keep on happening.

Once again, it is your job as the songwriter to recognize some event or fad, and then make your brilliant comment about it in a clever fashion, dazzling your audience with your wit and timing, with your cleverness (and even audacity) to push your agenda of absurdity into a song. If it works, you could have a smash, No. 1 seller. If it doesn't work, then you still made the effort. You did your job.

Political Songs, Timely Songs from the News, Songs of Social Significance

One hundred forty-three other writers already wrote a song about a particular recent "event," and that's just in one week. What are you going to do with it? In truth, these kinds of songs are difficult to get recorded, but it does happen. Politics, events, and songs have mixed successfully in the past. Anti-war, pro-war, anti-hunger, anti-racist, pro-love—all have had their day. Airplane crashes and train wrecks, sinking ships, racing motorcycles, speeding cars— each and every one chasing the No. 1 spot on the charts. Can it happen again? You betcha!

CHAPTER 7

Demos

I can't write about pitching songs without bringing up the subject of demos. There is a lot of controversy about demos and how simple or how elaborate they should be for your presentation. In my own career, I've had song demos that were a piano and vocal (or a guitar and vocal) and got them recorded, but that was early on. In almost all cases, the demos I produced were a combination of guitar(s), bass, drums, keyboards, vocal, background vocals and overdubs of guitar, and sometimes other instruments.

You are going to hear as many opinions about demos as there are music publishers, song pluggers, songwriters, producers, and artists. Here's how to structure a demo that will help you with your presentation.

> ▸ Very few producers, or any people on the list, will hear a recordable song with a simple demo of guitar or piano and vocal. Period.
>
> ▸ Those that do hear a hit song in that raw stage are still going to miss a few.
>
> ▸ Why take a chance on missing out?

As the use of home studios has become commonplace, more sophisticated demos have emerged. Consequently, over the past 20 years, music publishers, producers, and artists rarely have the opportunity to hear songs in the raw. Their ears are not tuned to the guitar-vocal and, frankly, most of them lack the imagination, skill, training, and experience to hear an arrangement in their head. There are exceptions, of course, but don't count on having the luck to be sitting opposite one of those rare birds.

My suggestion is to *make the best demos you can*. If you have a home studio, great! Even better, go into a studio and hire some demo musicians and produce your songs yourself. That is an art form unto itself. For economic reasons, the demo must be laid down fast. Get the hottest, most experienced musicians you can. If you have charts, send them to the musicians so they can review them ahead of time. It will all pay off with your end results.

As an example, I used the savviest professional musicians in town. Many times over the years, we laid down tracks in one take. We would record 10 or 12 songs in three or four hours. Sometimes, it went longer. These musicians had never heard the songs before they walked into the studio. We did "head arrangements." Decisions were made in a minute. Most of the time, the demos worked. Then we would lay down the vocals and background.

The background singers are very important. Again, they have to "get it" really fast, work out the parts, and be creative. Many times, the writer was an excellent singer for the lead vocal. That is not always so. It's a creative call.

You do not have the luxury of agonizing over the production. It's "down and dirty" compared to producing a master recording, but do not settle for anything except the best results. Keep your demo standards high.

It is really about what the cost is. The reality is that many of these songs will never be recorded. So you must keep your costs down. This is a practical approach, and you won't go broke by being prudent.

- When a song was cut, many record producers copied my demos.
- They were head arrangements that we did in the studio in 15 minutes or less.
- In other words, we laid down the road map on how the song should be recorded for a master recording.
- If this happens to you, don't take it the wrong way. They just flattered you by copying your style for your song.
- The bottom line is that you got a recording. It is your career.

As a writer, you have to decide which song or songs you are going to demo, and which songs *demand* to be demo'd and are worthy of backing with your hard-earned cash. You are putting a lot on the line each and every time you go into the studio to record your songs, so the process needs to be given a lot of careful thought and consideration about just what the *chosen* will be.

Any Fool Can Go into a Studio and Spend Money

Most songwriters fall into a bad habit when choosing the songs they are going to pitch and demo. Sometimes they feel that the last song they wrote is their best song. For the most part, that isn't true, but the writer thinks it is. When writers would pitch songs to me, I always asked that they pitch me at least one older song. Guess what? Many times, I took the song that was an older piece of material. That's because it was brand new to me.

You must be as objective as possible when selecting which songs to demo. This can be a tough situation, and you are going to have to figure it out yourself by trial and error. Nobody else can decide for you. Here are a few things to remember when producing your demo.

HOT TIP

- This is not a master.

- This is a demo.

- It won't be perfect!

- This is a demo.

- The recording should show off the song, suggest a direction.

- That's why it's called a demo.

- It's not about "perfect" vocals—it's about the song.

- You don't want it to be off-key or off-pitch; that will grate on the listener's nerves.

- It's a demo and the people you are playing it for know that.

- Be smart.

- Be creative.

- Learn to work fast and make decisions in the studio.

- Making demos is an art.

- It's a demo.

Along with your hard-earned money begging to be spent, your songs are burning a hole in your pocket waiting to be recorded. Remember this (and I can't say it enough): any fool can go into the studio and pay big bucks to record a bad bunch of songs. So learn to live with your material for a while before you go into the studio. Think about it.

HOT TIP

- After you have completed a song, put it away for 30 to 60 days.

- Write more songs.

- Put a future listening date of 60 days on your calendar. Now play your "hit song" again.

- By this time, your excitement and emotions should not be so wrapped up in the song.

- How does it sound now?

- Does it hold up for you, or is it not as hot as you thought?

- You can try to fix it or file it away for later reference.

I know many writers who follow these steps. It seems to work for them. The point is that you need to work and polish your song. Go over it line by line and ask yourself, "How can I say that better?" Your song is not finished until you lay it down as a demo. Even then, it can be changed.

All of this work is leading toward a better chance of having your song cut. I know you are going to hear stories like, "I wrote that song in ten minutes." Sure, and it's probably true that they wrote it in ten minutes. At least that was the conscious thought process at work. In such cases, I believe they have been writing that song for a long time in their subconscious. Writing is a nonstop operation. Songwriters are always looking for ideas, and the subconscious works its mystery. So one day, you can say, "I wrote that hit song in ten minutes." Cool. But you'll know how long it really took—perhaps two years.

What does this have to do with getting your songs recorded? Everything! The better your song is written, the better your chances of getting a recording. It all ties in with a big red bow.

Song Casting: Who Is Going to Record My Song?

HOT TIP

You are planning a song assault on R. Producer for Miss Golden Pipes. The same producer cut her past few albums. This can be good news for you. If you do not already have the recordings, you need to get your hands and ears on them. Listen to them a few times. Push yourself. You are a professional writer. Now get a pen and paper and break down each song by writing down the chords for each. String the chords for each song together, as though it were one long song, or look at the songs online and analyze their chord patterns. Do that for all of the recordings. A pattern should emerge.

Most producers and artists favor certain chord progressions, as do most songwriters. So you are going to favor the producer's or artist's favorite chord patterns by writing your song built around some of his or her favorite changes, with just slight variations. This takes some work. If you can't do this, find someone who can.

You are not done yet. Now, check out the lyrics online: What are the general themes of these songs? What are the standout lines, words, phrases, and what I call "phrase throws"?

Next, write down those words and phrases. Write the line that is a "throw the pencil in the air" line—a "Wow, I can't believe I wrote that!" line. Now analyze the line and general direction of the song. Is it a love song? An unrequited love song? A cheating song? A story song? Ah-ha! You have a direction. You have a chord pattern you know *they* will like. Can you write about the same theme sideways and upside down, and be original in the lyric content? That's your dilemma. That is your job. So knuckle down and get to work being a songwriter. Let's hear it!

A Very Stylized Demo

Next, you cut your demo to fit the artist or producer. Try to find a demo singer who sounds like Miss Golden Pipes, but not quite as good. Downplay the vocal. You want to give just a hint of Miss Golden Pipes. Many successful writers or publishers have a male vocal and a female vocal demo. This is psychological. R. Producer and Miss Golden Pipes hear your song and somewhere in back of their collective brain is the thought, "Hey, we can nail this sucker for sure." The competition is in your favor. Yeah! It works. (See more on song casting in chapter 10, p. 37.)

The Real Insider Information

CHAPTER 8

Pitching Songs and Goofing Off

Pitching songs is hard work, if you do it right. Unfortunately, it's very easy to make an excuse, or many excuses, for yourself and goof off for a few hours of the day. Let's look at the excuses:

It's Monday, so I'll give them a chance to get going and catch up. Besides, I didn't make the copies yet.

Tuesday: not a good day—they are really busy on Tuesdays. Maybe they are in staff meetings (and I didn't make the labels yet). Wednesday: they are out playing golf (besides, I need mailers). Thursday: it's almost the end of the week and I don't feel like going to the post office. Friday: well, if I get them on the phone today, they'll forget it by Monday. I'll call 'em up on Monday. Besides, I heard they don't want any more songs for now. Monday: I have to go to the market and then write with some guy I just met, so I can't make a call today. Besides, I am writing a new song today.

Think ...

▸ You can make all the excuses in the world for not picking up a phone.

▸ This is your career.

▸ You should be feeling great about it at this point because you are going to make a call that could change your life.

▸ Read the trade magazines and take notes. By setting a specific time to do this every week you are creating a positive work ethic for yourself to succeed as a songwriter.

▸ Package your songs. Do not buy one envelope at a time; instead, buy two dozen. Have your labels already done. Have a rough draft of the note you wish to enclose at the ready.

Or, if you're sending MP3s, be sure that the person you're sending them to will accept files in that format. The usual presentation guidelines apply: three songs only and inclusion of all pertinent information.

▸ Now you are treating your career as though it means something.

▸ It is your career.

▸ The truth is, you need to create a schedule. Monday is contact day. Make phone calls to record companies. Call for two hours. If you make one new contact a week for 50 weeks, you now have 50 new chances for getting a recording. And that's just on Monday. What about the rest of the week? Just do it. This is a business.

▸ Work it like a business, a job.

▸ Try saying "Oh, I don't feel like it today" on any other job, and you'll get fired.

Pitching songs is one of the most competitive of all careers. Hundreds of writers are trying to get to that "hot" producer/manager/artist/publisher. Don't fall for the cop-out of "I'm a creative person and I can't deal with the business end." That is pure B.S. All successful artists are driven and work hard at promoting their creations. They may not even be as talented as you are, but they persist and never give up.

Take a long look at the history of painters, sculptors, actors, singers, and songwriters. All of them are artists. These people have tremendous egos and are not shrinking violets. Don't be your own worst enemy. It's okay to have an ego; just keep it in check when you should. Use your common sense.

CHAPTER 9

Be Prepared

First, always have at least one song on you at all times. At *all* times. No matter where you are going. You never know whom you are going to run into. I have run into artists and producers and publishers in the most unlikely spots, such as other people's offices or hallways, the movies, on a trail while hiking, grocery stores, flea markets, concerts, parties, award shows, dog shows, restaurants, fast-food joints, airports, and even other countries. You get the idea.

Your package, your creation, your song, should be presented in a professional wrapper. Always include a lyric sheet (typed) with the name of the song you're submitting and your name, email address, and phone number. Your MP3 or CD should have the name of the song and your name, phone number, email, and home address on it, and remember to enclose a stamped, self-addressed envelope. Do not get cute with colors. You can include a short, to-the-point note saying that your song is for a certain artist and you hope to hear back from them. Carry a "one letter covers all" with your CD.

Here's a sample letter (short, sweet, to the point):

Dear Mr. R. Producer,

Enclosed is one song I feel is perfect for Miss Golden Pipes. The song is "Number One Hit." I'm looking forward to hearing from you soon.

A stamped, self-addressed return envelope is included.

Best regards,
Mr./Ms. S. Writer
Phone number/email
Address

Casting the Song

How to Make Contact — Unraveling the Mystery

Your song is ready to pitch. Fine! Now you must study who would be the best person to record it—and why! This is called "casting." For instance, you determine that the Tall Texas Country Guy would be perfect for your song. Check out his last album. See if he wrote all the songs, or if "outside" writers and music publishers were used. If outside writers are involved, then you have a shot. If you do not see outside writers, then perhaps you need to back off and look into another artist. If there are more than two other writers, you might be on the right track.

Billboard magazine (www.billboard.com) is your bible. It can give you the information you need, such as who produced the Tall Texas Country Guy's single. In *Billboard* and on the Web, you can find out the name of his producer, who his manager is, and who is his agent. These are all potential contacts for your song pitch. Start a file right now on who these people are. Add phone numbers and email addresses as you gather them.

Next, how do you track down these folks? The telephone and the Web are still your best tools. For example, if your artist is a country singer and he is on Hillbilly Records, it's an easy task to get the company's phone number.

Call them. Most companies have automated prompters; find a way to bypass them. A receptionist will answer. Ask for the producer by name.

Sometimes the producer will have an office at the record company. If so, you will be asked to state the nature of the call and your name. You answer that you are Mr. S. Writer and that you are a professional writer. Like magic, you are put through. Be ready for a fast conversation. "Hi, I'm S. Writer; are you going to be producing Miss Golden Pipes this time around?" "Yes, I am," answers the producer. "Great—I believe I have the perfect song for her. Is it okay if I send you the song? I will only send one song." "Sure, that would be fine," he replies. Then ask if there is a special address or code you should put on your envelope. Ask if sending an MP3 file would be okay. Try to find out when recording is going to start. If you are living in the area, drop off your package faster than Superman could. You might try for a meeting, but don't count on getting one. The record producer wants to hear your song first, and that takes about three minutes. A meeting is at best a half hour. That can be tough.

He or She Doesn't Have an Office Here ...

If the producer does not have an office at the record company, ask how you can contact him or her. The person assisting you may or may not have the number handy. If by chance they have the number, then call the producer directly. If they don't have a contact number, ask the name of the producer's production company. If they don't have any of that information, ask if there is a person at the record company who could listen to your song, like someone in the A&R department. If they say yes, pay attention to the name and how and in what format they want the song. Then send it. You don't stop there.

Continue to pursue the producer and the production company. Sometimes just by calling 4-1-1 information or Googling, you can find a producer's phone number, and contact information for a lot of other people you are trying to contact.

Somewhere, you will get the number. After all, other people have to be able to get in touch with this person. Keep at it. It isn't fun; it's a drudge. It is your career on which you are working. You build your file one name at a time.

> ▸ Keep in mind that the artist and the producer need hit songs, great material, and original material.
>
> ▸ They need it more than you need to get a recording.
>
> ▸ They must perpetuate their careers.

Here Is One of the Fastest Learning Curves Ever

Scene: You have an appointment with Mr. B. Shot, record producer/music publisher/manager/VIP. You are ushered into the inner sanctum of the above-mentioned deity. You make a little small talk. You hand over your "love child/song." Mr. B. Shot takes your CD or flash drive in his hands and slips it into the machine. Meanwhile, you can hardly believe it. Here you are! Mr. B. Shot is going to hear your creation, your for-sure hit song.

"Do do do ron ron whomp whomp—my heart flips for ya, darling …" The speaker system must have a problem. "Gee," you think, "I thought his sound system would be better than that. My song sounds funny. I wish I hadn't brought this song. It's not really so good after all. Geez, I wish I was only about two inches tall and I could just slip under the door."

I guarantee that this will happen to you at some point. You will recover, and you will learn from it—really fast.

Your Job as the Songwriter Is to Make the Listener Care

Make me care. Make me give a damn. A lyric line has to make a connection with the listener. For me to be impressed, the song has to slap me around the room—not just once, but about ten times. Then the song must, has to, do a repeat performance the next time I listen to it. And every time I listen to it I have to say to myself, "That is outstanding!" If you don't make me care, it's a pass.

The hardest thing is to write a song that cuts through to a person's emotions, heart and soul, and brain. Then the commercial aspect raises its ugly, or beautiful, head. Songwriters write for themselves; they express with words their innermost private feelings, which end up being shouted to the world. Sometimes it is hard for you, the writer, to let go and feed the hungry masses that will cling to your every word. Some writers don't like "sharing" those private moments. That is a hurdle only you can jump.

As a music publisher, producer, or artist, your duty is to recognize the message of the material and nurture it to a life of its own though the artist.

I Don't Write Commercial Songs

How many times have I heard, "I don't write commercial songs"? You have no idea how many times I have heard that said. My answer, "Oh, really? Then I guess this meeting is over."

There is nothing wrong with a "commercial" song. It just means more people relate to it, as opposed to a song that only ten people on the planet like. You may say, "I only write personal songs, so nobody understands my songs." Maybe, maybe not! Personal songs? Have I got news for you—*all* songs are personal. Feelings are universal. You are not the lone wolf of the universe. If you have skill as a lyric writer, your deeply personal song is going to touch millions of other lone wolves. You are their spokesperson, saying what they can identify with but can't put into words.

HOT TIP

▸ There is no such thing as a song that is too personal or private.

▸ If you don't write commercial songs, then why are you trying to get a recording?

CHAPTER 11

Tip Sheets

Song Plugger Publications and Tip Sheets—

Whatzup in the World of Record Production

Tip sheets can be either good, so-so, or bad news. They are usually based on one or two people gathering information about who is producing which artist for what company and when. Tip sheets also list what type of song is being looked for and the name of the person you should contact. The charge for these tip sheets, however, is often high.

Should you subscribe to one of these sheets? Short answer: Why not? What's funny to me is that most writers and almost all music publishers deny that they use tip sheets; it's as if they feel that their professionalism is somehow challenged by the fact that they subscribe.

From time to time, any given record company will put out a sheet of which artists they are trying to find material for and what kinds of songs are needed. These sheets are the toughest for those not yet in the "club" to get a hold of. They are tough because they tend to go out only to a select few of the professionals they know, such as certain writers and music publishers. Sometimes you can get your hands on one that is several months old. That's okay—you know what to do with the information, you are building a file.

Here's the Deal ...

Here's what I feel is the key element with tip sheets. You can go through the motions of pitching your songs on the current issue; however, the contact information is of key importance for future reference.

HOT TIP

Suggestions for using tip sheet information:

▸ Put that info in your contact files, along with the appropriate information. Then, flag those new contacts to remind you to make your inquiries in about a month. Put a prompt on your computer.

▸ If you have only an address and no phone number, call 4-1-1 for information or search for the number on the Web. Now you have the name of a person or company and their address, email, and phone number.

▸ Thirty days after a particular tip sheet issue comes out, the rush of calls and songs pouring into the contact person's office should have slowed down to a trickle.

▸ At this point you may have a better shot at getting heard.

▸ Send one song.

▸ Flag your files from the tip sheet for 90 days after the tip sheet was issued, and call the contact person when the time has elapsed. At that time, ask whom they are producing currently and what kinds of songs are needed.

This should be an ongoing process for you. Some tip sheet publications come out every two weeks; others come out once a month. If you do your job and contact these people, you can get your song recorded or, at least, considered.

Look at the cost of the publication. In a year of pitching, if you get one song cut and a halfway decent-selling artist records the song, you now have made many times your money back, and you have a real copyright!

Keep up that contact list. Keep calling to see whom your contacts are recording. Some producers have many artists lined up for future recording dates.

After a year of gathering tip sheet information, you should be able to compile an impressive list of contacts. Just this one list could keep you busy if you follow through. Over the years, I've had several cuts from tip sheet info, and a few of these cuts were even with major artists. That's the so-so and the good news.

The bad news is that whoever is gathering the information and publishing the current tip sheets determines how good the information is. Sometimes all you see are the same names with different projects. This isn't good for you as far as your own files. It also shows that the publishers of the sheet are not widening their contacts.

Many producers, managers, and A&R people do not like to give information for tip sheets. They get inundated with material, most of it bad to worse. They deal with rank amateur writers and rude, unprofessional people, so why should they voluntarily subject themselves to this torture?

This is why your package has to look professional. And this is why, when you call and talk to someone, you must have your thoughts in order. Write down your points. Make it short and sweet. You do not have to mention the tip sheet publication. This is your career and you don't have to tout the sheet info.

How do you find tip sheets? Do a search online. Also, many songwriting organizations can lead you to tip sheets. Talk with other writers about the sheets. Note that some of them come and go like the wind.

The Recording Studio

Songs are recorded in studios. Studios have studio managers or owners. Studios have engineers. You can get a meeting with these people; it isn't difficult to do. Engineers are your best bet because few people ever want to meet with them. Tell him or her that your meeting will take 15 minutes. That's it. In your meeting, explain that you are a songwriter and that the engineer is in a position of "knowing all about what's going on in the studio." That is, who is recording, who the producer is, who the artist is, and what kinds of songs are being recorded. All the engineer has to do is pass on this info to you, the songwriter.

Then, based on what the engineer has told you, you will package one or two songs and drop the package off at the studio. The engineer tells the producer or artist that a writer left this package for them. The engineer never has to reveal that he or she knows you. So it's no problem for them—nothing will come back to haunt them if your songs are not up to par.

Now for the good part. If your engineer buddy passes the song to an artist who cuts it, then part of your deal is that you will pay the engineer 10 percent of the income from that recording for one year, or however long you think will work. Put it in writing, with the name of the song and the artist. Date it and honor your commitment. As a result, you may end up with several leads a year from a sharp, on-the-ball engineer.

Now, imagine that you have a dozen engineers lined up with this deal. It's a win-win for you and them. This is a legit proposition. This is legal. This is doing business and getting your song exposed and recorded. Over a period of time, you can build this up to 30 or 40 or more engineers.

This proposition will work with studio managers and owners as well. Do it. You have nothing to lose and a career to make happen. It works. Now read this again. Make your first meeting tomorrow. Better yet, make it right now.

If you have 12 engineers and 30 studio managers working for you through this deal, you have multiplied your inside information by 100 percent over and above your competition.

Secretaries and Assistants

For you, the songwriter, developing a good relationship with secretaries and assistants can be your lifeline, your only connection for contacting and communicating with the inner sanctum. Sometimes you can learn more from them about a project than from the producer or the artist. What to do about these special, magic people who are the workers?

Here are a few pointers to remember when dealing with them: Be nice. Be professional. Don't hit on them. Ask how they are. Ask if they have a few minutes to help you out by answering some questions. If they say they are really busy, respect that and say you'll call back later the next day. Don't hassle them or make them mad at you.

Treat these secretaries and assistants the way you would like to be treated. Try to put yourself in their place. Secretaries and assistants are usually very busy and are a harried group. If you can make yourself known to them, they can help you more than almost anyone else can.

Never underestimate the power of these people. They can get you an appointment, or they can trash your package and file it in the well-known "round file." Cultivate a relationship with them. Write down their names. In the course of a conversation, find out if they have kids, are married, or any other personal information. These are important additions to your files and should go into your records of information pertaining to the producer and artist.

In my career, I have been fortunate to meet and hire some great secretaries and assistants. Whether it was my own secretary, who had an ear to the ground, or the secretary of a producer, a record company big shot, an artist, or an organization that believed in me—the publisher—that information was valued and appreciated by me. Sometimes a secretary would give me some information about a writer and would suggest I see them. I always paid attention to them. Many times they were right. I have also met a few secretaries and assistants that were awful, and there's no telling what damage they caused to the unknowing writer and me.

When a secretary goes to bat for you, or you suspect that she or he did, be sure to call and thank that person when you get an appointment or a callback from the person you're pitching to. If you feel comfortable about it, send a thank you note. Sometimes it's even okay to send flowers or a similar gift as a sincere thank you. I have met with secretaries for a professional thank you business lunch, given them tickets to concerts, or sent flowers, gift baskets, wine, albums, T-shirts, hats, and other promo items of the artist with whom I was working. Play it by ear and use your own discretion.

I know from long experience that just being aware of these professional secretaries and assistants by remembering their names and acknowledging them and their contribution to the process is part of being professional. Not only is this smart business, but it's also one of the ways that business is done. In most cases, all these people deserve a thank you of some kind. After all, everyone likes to be recognized as a person, as someone who contributed. They don't have to go out of their way for you, and it's good policy to acknowledge whatever contribution they have made in getting you "in." They helped you out. No one does this alone.

If you follow some of these suggestions, you'll learn things that will get your songs cut. It sure makes things more pleasant in this "turndown" business.

You may also learn that Ms. Sec is leaving to go to another gig. After Ms. Sec starts this new job, send a note of congratulations or a small but appropriate gift. Wait a few weeks and then call to see what's up. Many times, by keeping up with people, it can be good for you as they get promoted.

Take care of business, and the business will take care of you. Pay attention to the details and remember it is a people connection, so connect. It's your career.

CHAPTER 14

Playing Your Song for a Contact

The publisher/artist/producer/manager/contact must have the talent and ability to recognize an original piece of work—one would think. One of the songs I played for many producers and friends was met with "My gawd! That song is fantastic—you'll get it cut in a heartbeat" and "Wow, how come no one has cut that song yet?"

Many producers "held" the song. I kept right on pitching it. At one point, I was going to have four or five recordings of the song. All of this took about four months. Even though it had some lines I had never heard in a song before and it worked and did all the right things, had a fantastic hook, and so on, no one jumped at it or fell all over themselves trying to cut it. Finally, it was cut. The song went to No. 1. It has been covered several times over, even as a country duet.

After the song was on the charts and zooming toward No. 1, here's what happened: *Ring, ring.* "Hello, this is Dude." The voice through the receiver says, "Hey man, how come you didn't let me hear that song?" "Hmmm," I answer, "Let's see, Mister B.S. Producer—according to my handy phone file, I sat in your office on August 12 at 1 p.m. and played *only* this song for you, and you turned it down." "Oh." Or, someone calls and says, "Say, you never let me get a chance to get into the studio with that song." My answer: "I couldn't wait for you to make up your mind. I left messages for you, but you never called me back." (Being a mind reader is not one of my main talents.)

The point: After a song has been recorded and is on the charts and taking off like a rocket, after all the trades are reporting that the radio stations are going ape over it, anybody can tell it's a hit. All of a sudden everyone recognized it as a super song, and they all knew it was going to be a hit. Except they all sat on their respective butts for months at a time, before the song was recorded and released, and did nothing. Nothing. Followers lose.

Let's go back to the problem of kennel blindness, discussed in Chapter 3. It's a fact that the producer or publisher may be kennel blind as well. This is a major hurdle to overcome, and one you cannot possibly foresee. Or the individual may also be a writer who doesn't like your chord changes or the way you wrote a certain line because that's not the way he or she would have said it. Or they just like certain kinds of songs. Or they really aren't good at being a song evaluator. You have to love songs and appreciate what they say and how they say it to be a "real" producer or music publisher. Sadly, these people are hard to find, but they do live in the industry. They are not a myth.

No one will always hear a hit, and that's the other side of the coin. Many producers and publishers will tell you that they never passed on a hit song. That's a heavy load of bull. They might not even remember it if you had played it for them. Passing on an album cut is easy. At some point, once in a while, *everyone* misses a hit.

Contact Has Been Made!

You've been fortunate enough to get the attention of a producer, music publisher, or VIP (and that is because you used the info in this book). They contact you about your song, but they tell you they are going to pass. However, they would like to hear more of your material. Great—you have made contact! Don't blow it.

Tell the producer (or whoever the contact is) that you will get her some more material soon. Then do it in a heartbeat. I prefer to submit one song at a time, unless the contact specifies that he or she wants more than that. My suggestion is to send no more than three songs.

Your contact passes. But he or she knows who you are. Don't blow it. Wait three or four weeks, and then send one more song. Call first to let them know that you are sending it. Keep a record of when and what you have sent to this person. Keep up this contact. Don't bug the hell out of them, but be consistent, like once every three to six weeks. You now have one contact, the first of many to come. This is the way you build your contact list: File the phone number in your computer's phone number program. Write down the following.

- Contact name and company

- Address

- Email address

- Name of the artist for whom you submitted a song

- Name of the song(s) you have submitted

- Date you sent the song(s)

- Date they made contact with you

- Name of the assistant, the secretary, and any other names (along with respective job titles) of people who could be important to you

• Name of the studio where they are recording

- Name of the recording engineer

- Keep a record of which songs they turned down.

- Have a calendar and mark down the week you should call again.

- Put a prompt on your computer, with the week you should call.

Billboard and Other Trade Magazines

Keep up with the trade publications. If a contact moves on to another company or starts up a production company, your information will be up-to-date. Keep up with this person, no matter where they go. Some of these relationships can go on for many years. Never give up on getting a song recorded with your contact.

The trades:

Billboard magazine (www.billboard.com)
Music Connection (www.musicconnection.com)

Publications like *Billboard* and *Music Connection* are important because you get to see pictures of people like R. Producer, I. Manage, or T. Agent. Develop a memory for faces and names, because it could come in handy. Here's why: although you might never have met Mr. M. Publisher (pick the VIP of your choice), you know what he looks like from a few photos you have seen in the trades (you can also find photos on the Web in places such as Google Images).

Let's say that you now have the phone numbers and the extensions of Mr. R. Producer or Ms. I. Manage. But after a few calls or several attempts to reach them (always keep a log of your calls), it seems obvious that you won't be able to get these VIPs on the phone. So go into off-hours mode. The unconventional move is called "Call 'em late!"—perhaps, at 8 p.m. or 9 p.m. I have used this ambush tactic many times in my career, and you would be amazed at how many times the VIP answers the phone. When they answer, don't say, "Geez, I was just going to leave a message." Sound professional and make it short and sweet. Make the best of it. Calling on some holidays works also. I have worked in my office on many holidays and have reached other professionals getting in a little quiet time.

HOT TIP

- Because you are prepared and have your demo always at the ready, you can make a positive and confident approach.

- I know this works because I have done this many times in my career.

- Walk up to R. Producer and say, "Hello, Record, nice to see you again; we met very briefly at the BMI/ASCAP/Whatever Awards Dinner last year.

- If he or she says, "I wasn't there," then your comeback is, "Well, I must have my events mixed up. But I do have a piece of material I think you may like," and hand him or her your package.

- His or her hand will automatically accept it.

- Tell him or her, "It's only one song. Nice to see you again," Shake his or her hand and walk away.

- It will work.

- It worked each and every time I did it.

CHAPTER 16

Travel

So you're going to Nashville (or L.A., or New York) for a week to pitch your songs in person. Good for you—you're going to go see the heart of the business. Hopes and high expectations are up; they should be.

HOT TIP

My rule could be your rule:

▸ Don't go to these music cities during any big or major music events.

▸ Reason? You and 30,000 other writers and artists have the same idea.

▸ Do not go the week of any holiday.

Music professionals take big-time advantage of long holiday weekends by adding a few extra days at each end. They will deny doing that.

Make your appointment ahead of time with any publishers, producers, managers, agents, and artists. You don't need to mention that you are *not* already in town. Here's the reason: "Oh, you're coming in over the weekend? Why don't you call me when you get here, and we'll set up a time then."

If you agree to that, what happens is this:

> "Hi, B. Shot Producer, I'm in town now. When can I see you? You said to call when I was in town."

> "Golly, H. Writer, I've had to do some schedule changes. You wouldn't happen to be able to make it next week, would you? I'm pretty free then!"

That's an old trick to get out of out-of-town writer appointments. This way, they are not the bad guys. They are just very busy, and it's not their fault. It's your fault.

Many writers wait until they are in town and start calling for appointments first thing Monday morning.

> "Hi, I'm in town for the week. Could I get a meeting?"

> "Wow, man, I'm in the studio most of the week; what does next Tuesday look like for you?"

> "Man, I'm only here for this week."

> "Oh, too bad. Call me next time you're in town." You are out in the cold. Poor planning on the writer's part! Work smart!

That's why you fudge your schedule a bit. That's called doing good business. Oh sure, if you wait until you are in their city, you will get a few appointments. But you need to utilize your precious time to the utmost. It's your career!

You could go for two weeks. You have to get every shot in that you can, by using your time wisely.

Go and meet with the reps from ASCAP, SESAC, and BMI and ask them questions. Visit anyone and everyone you know. Call everyone you know in town. Find out the "in" places where the pros and the writers hang out.

Check to find any professional organization meetings, like the Association of Independent Music Publishers in Los Angeles and New York, the California Copyright Conference in Los Angeles, or the Nashville Songwriters Association. If you've done your homework, you just might run into someone that you'll recognize. The "in" places are not just where they play music; they also include breakfast and lunch places, even dinner and the hip watering holes. Don't be shy! Be professional.

Plan your trip. Arm yourself the best you can and be ready to change your plan in a moment's notice. Don't forget anyone or anything. Write down your plan and follow it, but be flexible.

Have fun and enjoy your experience. You should learn a lot from your trip. Take detailed notes; keep a log of all your meetings and where, when, and with whom you met. Make additions to your files for future contacts. Start early in the morning with breakfast and look around to see if you recognize anyone at all. There are occasions when I went to three places for breakfast. Same deal at lunch and dinner. Many times more "biz" is done in these casual settings than anywhere else. Sometimes you can work in a little sightseeing (such as visiting the Country Hall of Fame in Nashville). That is a distant second best to your mission! Better to go home with a cut!

Think a Minute Before You Act

I know I've preached about taking every opportunity to pitch your songs and to always have them at the ready. In some instances, though, it's best to ask yourself whether a particular situation is the right time to pitch or not. For example, I saw a star go into the bathroom at a function. It just so happened I was heading that way, too. So was a very desperate songwriter; I think he figured he had a captive audience. While the star was otherwise occupied sitting on the throne, this desperate writer jumps up, hangs onto the partition, and tries to hand his CD to the star. I couldn't believe it! The loud yelling from the star should have been recorded. The star chasing the idiot writer out of the room was just perfect. I left also. I didn't want to be linked to that deal in any way whatsoever. It's funny to tell about, but think before you act.

If you see someone eating dinner or lunch, wait at least until they have finished their meal, or hit them before the meal is served. Pick your shots. Sometimes when you run into these VIPs, it just isn't right to pitch a song. You have to know when the right time to approach them is. Think for a minute. Don't be rude.

At a club one night, I overheard an artist saying that he was going to be at a certain place at about five in the morning with his bus. It was the only chance he would have to pick up some gear in person. Guess who was there at five in the morning with songs in hand? Guess who finally had two and a half hours of sleep that night, after we put together a demo?

CHAPTER 18

Contacts—Keep Making New Ones

Early in my career, after working for about five years at pitching songs, I had collected a sizeable list of names, addresses, and phone numbers, some of which were (at the time) almost impossible to get your hands on. Sometimes you help out a buddy by giving out contact info, but for the most part, you should play it close to the vest.

So, because of this important list, a very big publisher once offered me a substantial sum of money for my phone list. What would you do? I turned it down. Isn't this list of names and numbers a part of my livelihood? I worked hard and smart for this list.

The Importance of Making New Contacts

HOT TIP

The truth raises its "ugly" head—the importance of making new contacts! Why is it so important to make new contacts constantly? Because almost immediately your list starts to lose importance through old-fashioned attrition. It loses at the rate of about one person a week. That's right, one a week. The person who is impossible to get an appointment with today won't even be around a year later, or may not be working in the business.

The rarified air of big publishers, producers, artists, and managers is difficult to sustain year after year. In reviewing old daybook calendars and computer printouts and consulting with friends in the business, I have come to the unfortunate conclusion that a good run for a hot producer and artist lasts about five years. The same goes for the publishers, managers, and even songwriters. I repeat: that's a good run. It could even be only two years. Of course there are exceptions, but those are rare.

At first, the attrition will be subtle. If you keep phone records in a log, go back a few years and you will be amazed at the names you find that are no longer viable. They are gone, and they were big deals. So make new contacts all the time. In spite of the good run and then falling off the cliff to oblivion, many of these people do come back three or four or even ten years later. If you try your best to keep up with them, it might just pay off for you in the long term.

You've Got to Know the Right People

Business is not only what you know and what you do. You've heard "Politics—it's not *what* ya know, it's *who* ya know!" Well, that's partly true. "Getting songs recorded is all politics"—that's partly true, as well. So what?

Business is a combination of politics and who you know. "Music Business!" Sound familiar? It's the way we all describe what we do. "I'm in the music biz." "I'm in the entertainment business."

I believe that if you are already in this business and making a living at it, then you are a lucky person. If you are selling trucks and making a living at it, you are also one lucky person.

The music business is a business first and foremost. We should call it "business music," because that's the way it really is. So what do you have to do? Meet people. If *your* product is better, then only you can promote it. Join every organization you can. Attend meetings. Get involved. That's politics. That's part of doing business. Some of the people you meet are going to be successful on any number of levels.

I recall being in a music-business seminar many years ago. An extremely successful songwriter and a legendary producer were the guest speakers. About 75 people were in the room. I still remember what the writer and the producer said: "Out of all the talent in this room, if we come back in 20 years to see who is still making a living in the music business, two of you will be left standing!" This is a sad but true fact. I am proud to say that I am one of the two who are left standing! And I remain friends with the famous songwriter.

It is all about meeting people. Call it politics, with a sneer, if you wish. However, that's the way it is. Be part of the community. That's politics.

More on Contacts— New and Newer

"You shouldn't take your song to him—he's a real jerk," says a colleague of yours. Consider this: take into account who is telling you not to pitch your song to this person. What is their motivation for telling you? Do they have a song on hold with that producer and they don't want your song to replace their song? This may sound a bit paranoid, but it's been known to happen. The more likely scenario is this: the person telling you not to see a certain producer (or whoever) could have had a bad experience, been turned down, felt slighted, been treated badly, or be paranoid. All of these things can and will happen to you.

My suggestion is to go and get a meeting and find out for yourself. After all, that was that songwriter's experience, not yours. Maybe it was just a personality clash, or maybe it was the songwriter him- or herself. Obnoxiousness runs on both sides of the street.

This very thing happened to me early in my career, and I stayed away from pitching my songs to this person. Then my brain kicked in, and I said to myself, "Wait a minute."

I got my meeting and the person in question and I got along just fine! Eventually, I got a song recorded with this person.

Now, this is not to say that you should take your songs *everywhere*. You want to make sure the person to whom you are taking your songs is a legit professional working in the business. Some so-called producers and record companies are really just "vanity" companies. They are in business to have *you* fund (that is, pay for) the recording of your song, then pay for the manufacturing, marketing, distribution, promotion, and so on. Learn to know the difference. Don't mix this up with a demo studio or producing a real demo.

Rude and Obnoxious

At some point, you will encounter the totally rude, arrogant know-it-all producer/artist/manager/A&R person, and you will have the good fortune to have landed an appointment with this genius. Keep one thing in mind: he is the genius, and you are the idiot! I say that with tongue firmly planted in cheek. You can be the judge.

Human nature dictates certain reactions in all of us. Follow me on this: You play your songs. The rude genius puts you down; he denigrates your demo. All in all, he is a real jerk. You have a few options: you can smile and nod, then leave and tell everyone that this person is a %*#&^$)@*#, or leave and kick cans, or tell him to shove it. Take the first option and don't burn bridges; you never know where this guy is going to turn up next.

Picking songs is a subjective process, and there is no need to be a rude jerk to the writer who has created what he or she thinks is a viable work. The song may be lousy and have problems, but there is no need to be nasty about it. I would hope the publisher/producer would have the expertise to point out in a constructive manner what he or she perceives as its flaws. Don't let these types of people ruin it for you. They are just one person. By the same token, you don't need to be nasty or defensive. Take the high road. *It's your career.*

A Meeting

Now, you are excited. You have a face-to-face appointment. How do you look? By that, I don't mean that you need to look like a star, but rather that your appearance can be a factor. Be clean and neat, maybe just a bit more upscale than normal. You don't need a business suit or dress.

Be on Time, Be on Time

Be a bit early, even ten minutes. Just be on time! Even when you are on time, you may have to wait. Don't take it personally. Many of the producers and A&R people are not all that professional themselves. That doesn't mean you can slack. Be on time! *It's your career!*

Important point: when the person with whom you are meeting turns down your song, don't argue. They have made a decision already; respect that! Your argument that it would work for so-and-so won't win them over. A sales pitch for your song won't work. The song must stand on its own. No amount of selling will change the song in the listener's ears.

On the other hand, if the person wants to hold the song and listen to it some more, you are in the door, thumbs-up. This is what you want. Don't hang out like you are old buds. Wind it up, and listen carefully to the words of the person with whom you are having the meeting. Take the hint—stand up and thank him or her for the meeting. Ask when you should check back, shake hands, and get out of Dodge.

Terminology

Every business has its own jargon. So you need to avoid saying things that tell the pro you don't know how the music biz ticks.

There are a few phrases you must absolutely not use. One phrase you don't ever want to use is "I want to *sell* my songs," or "I'm *selling* my song to you." Drop the word "sell." You are not selling anything. Not a thing. You especially are not "selling" your song. You do want the song *recorded* or *published!* The record company is the only one *selling* anything. When the record company sells the digital recording, the CD, or the DVD, that's one form of income for you. You are not selling anything. Using that word tells the pro that you really don't know what you are talking about!

Many years ago, it was common for a writer to "sell" a song for *x* number of dollars. What this meant varied from situation to situation. One scenario was that you wrote the song and another person or company bought it from you, and then slapped their name on the song. If that song sold millions, you got nothing! Why? Because you sold it outright (see the section "Writing for Hire" in Chapter 29).

Another practice was to sell your song and all future rights, but to credit you as the writer. You just never made any more money on it. All the money instead went to the entity that paid you a fee for your song. Hopefully, this practice is long gone, and you should just run from anyone who tries to *buy* your song.

You can learn more about how the business works by attending songwriter workshops, seminars, songwriter organizations and ASCAP, SESAC, and BMI seminars, and from many excellent books (see the "Appendices"). What you don't know can and will hurt you!

When You Are in the Middle of a Song Pitch

HOT TIP

At your pitch meeting, take a few more songs with you as backup. If the contact person asks if you have anything else, you can whip out your songs and say, "Sure, right here!"

It's a hard call if you should or should not volunteer that you have a few extra songs handy. That's a call you have to make based on the situation. Keep track of the time. A half hour is a long time for a busy producer or whomever. When the meeting is over, thank the person and leave.

If they are going to listen to your song later on, ask when you can check back with them—in a week, two weeks.

Now wait a week and check in. No answer? That's okay. Another week—ask if it is it a hold or a pass. Ask if you can leave off one more song. It won't hurt. Never give up on pitching your songs to this person. You never know whom they might be working with next. Be persistent. It might take years before you get a cut with this person, but don't give up.

Requests For Specific Song Types

The top songs over the years are not always upbeat and happy—often they are sad songs, unrequited love songs, lonely songs, she/he-left-me songs. Those are followed in popularity by "pedestal" love songs and unique-story songs. Producers and artists request happy, upbeat songs, which often are the hardest to write without sounding corny. Ask someone how they are feeling today. "Oh, I'm feeling really great, just super" is the answer. Ask them why, and they will rarely have a good explanation. Or if they do, it's a two-word reason—"Just because."

Ask the same question of someone else. If their response is, "I feel lousy, just terrible," they will then usually offer you a laundry list of problems.

Sad songs have been the biggest hit makers over the years. Sad songs are easier to write because we seem to be able to draw forth those emotions from our memory banks as they burst right to the surface. Everybody loves a clown, but the sad clown is the most popular.

What Is a Star, Really?

Being a popular personality is not as all-encompassing as you would think, nor is it what the film, TV, and video companies would like you to believe.

If a pop star sells 5 million records, that also means 295 million people did not like it (that's just in this country), were indifferent to it, or just don't have any idea who the pop star is. So keep things in perspective. Pop culture media and marketing lead us around by the nose, making us think that these people are everything there is to be in this world, when in fact they have very little to do with how we live and what we do. Many such personalities cannot keep a handle on that fact, and they become difficult to deal with. So, if you are confronted by one of these types and are treated like so much debris, just write it off to self-indulged stupidity. The ego is a strange partner.

My point is that this business is full of "stars," and the power that comes with popularity infects some beyond all common sense. Don't let those types ruin it for you. Because the flip side of this is that there are also stars who have a handle on what being a "name" means. These folks can be a delight to work with, and many of those relationships last for years.

That "Has-Been" Artist

Hey, hey, hey … has-beens (in whose eyes?) sometimes make comebacks. Or at least they might spike up the charts and sell a reasonable number of records. The bottom line is—it's a recording. So even if you don't make much money on a song, it is always nice to say, "I had a song cut by Mr. Name Artist," who everybody knows. That alone could get you an appointment in some cases. The people you're pitching to don't know when you had the cut. Think about it. I have had a few of those. You can, too.

Songwriter Songs

What are "songwriter songs"? When writers get together and play songs for each other, beware of the trap when other writers just fall all over your song. You have simply impressed a bunch of other writers. Okay, and *so*? Nashville, Los Angeles, and New York are loaded with these writers. This is known as a "songwriter's song," and most likely it will never be recorded. Exceptions do happen. These are great exercises and can lead you to creating that hit song. Confused by this statement? After a while you will hear them—songs that have great lines, detailed stories, and descriptive words, but that won't be recorded by any mainstream artist. They are so well crafted that they are almost perfect, but they are not commercial in the truest sense. Sometimes only writers or an intimate group get to hear them. Consider yourself lucky when you find yourself with such a group.

Pitching Against Type—the "Off Pitch"

Let me explain what I mean by an "off pitch." You have access to an artist. The word is that they are looking for an up-tempo song. Great! Supergood news, but you are not the lone songwriter riding to the rescue here. About 60 or 70 music publishers are going to pitch an average of two up-tempo songs each. That's 120 to 150 songs.

In addition, 100 to 200 songwriters are going to be pitching an average of two songs each. That's a potential of another 400 songs. Then there are perhaps 20 to 30 lawyers representing clients including publishers and songwriters—adding another 100 songs—each and every one of which is up-tempo! This does not include songs from friends and insider songs. The producer and artist are now exposed to approximately 650 songs, all up-tempo. After the first 150 to 200 songs are listened to (gag!), the producer and the artist are a bit numb. The songs start to sound alike, and they blend into one long never-ending sound.

Off pitch—what? We have just run down the numbers of songs that are going to this producer. All of them are up-tempo because that is what has been requested. You are going do something a bit different. Very different!

HOT TIP

You have a monster in your catalogue—a crushing power ballad. It's a fantastic song, a "hit-in-waiting" that the artist could nail.

Pitch it about two weeks after you feel the producer and artist have been sifting through the up-tempo songs and are about burned out on them. If you can reach them by phone, tell them you have a song they just have to hear. One song! Don't tell them it's a ballad.

Now, it had better be a killer ballad to back up this "off pitch." If it is in the upper 2 percent, you might just nail it. Do it. The worst they can do is pass on recording it.

Be bold, be gutsy. Be smart. Pitch it. This has worked for me; it can for you, too.

The off pitch does not always work, but it is just one more tool to put in your bag of song pitching. Always look to see if you think an off pitch might be right.

I Only Want a Known Artist to Cut My Songs

I can't begin to tell you how many times I've heard the above statement! Well, from one point of view, the idea makes a lot of sense, and if you have the opportunity, getting a star should always be your first choice. Makes sense to me. However, every one of these artists, these well-known artists, these hit-record artists, these very famous name acts, have one thing in common: at one time, they were all unknowns! I don't care who they are now, or how big they are. At one time, they were no more known than was your second cousin who worked at the garlic factory.

A Hit Song Doesn't Care Who Sings It

From time to time, you will become aware that some unknown "phantom artist" is looking for songs. Your reaction—negative: "I'm not going to waste my time and my song of the century on some unknown artist no one has ever heard of. I don't want to throw away my song and ruin my chances of getting it recorded by a 'real' artist later on down the pike."

What kind of thinking is this? *Wrong* thinking. Every artist was unknown at one time. Pitch your best songs to this unknown. If the artist records your song and nothing happens, a few things still could be in your favor: you'll have a better demo to pitch; the next time this "unknown" records, he or she will call you for songs; or, if nothing happens, it will not hurt your song.

If you are worried that having an unknown record your song will taint your chances of it becoming a major recording, you can say, "For all intents and purposes, this song has never been recorded by an artist." Or you can say a small or indie label cut the song, and even mention the name. I have never had this tactic backfire and always got the cut.

On the other side of this coin, your song breaks the artist! It's the single; at the least, it's on the album. *A hit song doesn't care who sings it.* Now you look like a genius. You have nothing to lose and a huge career move to gain. Go for it.

Pitching Directly to a Star

This does happen, and more often than you may think. Some stars are very good at knowing just what they are looking for. Have one to three songs at the ready. Some of these stars are gracious; some can be rude. Some of them don't have a clue. That's not different from pitching to anyone else, is it? Relax and be yourself. You will be okay. That "star" is a person who happens to need a *hit song* to further his or her career. You might have the answer. My suggestion is not to have any more than two or three songs on a CD. However, be ready to pitch any number of songs.

True story: I was pitching three songs to a hot top star, a legendary performer. My thinking was, "Well, I've got three shots here. I don't want to take up his time." I played the three songs; he passed on all of them. I opened up my briefcase to put the songs back and he said to me, "What's that in your case? More songs?" I replied yes and he said, "Well, why can't I hear those?" I answered with, "Well, I didn't think you would have the time for all these songs." The star looked at me and said, "I make a very good living singing songs, and if I can't take the time to listen to what you or anyone else has to offer, then I don't deserve to be in this business!"

I was stunned. In all, I played him 36 songs. He passed on them all for himself, but took one for another artist he was working with and they cut the song. To say the least, this was a refreshing experience. Just don't count on this kind of dedication. This was a rare occurrence. These sorts of meetings do take place. Enjoy the ride. Be calm, be yourself, and you may end up with a cut.

Your Song Is on Hold

"We are holding your song!" Your song is "on hold" by R. Producer. Congratulations. You just might get a song recorded.

A reality check is in order right now. It is possible that they will really record your song. Here's the way it works: in most cases, the producer will gather *x* number of songs to reevaluate and play for his artist. Many times the producer will play the songs for his inner circle of "yes, sirs" who have an agenda of their own, like, what about *their* songs?

Now let's say that your song survives the inner circle. The time line for the producer to find songs can be from several days to weeks to months. He may grow tired of your song, find flaws he didn't notice before, or, for whatever reason, feel that the song just does not hold up for him. Or maybe the artist just doesn't like it. Conjure up your own suspicious reasons why your song doesn't get recorded.

However, you don't know all this is going on. You are crossing your fingers and telling people that your song is—those magical words—*on hold*. It's practically recorded.

If Your Song's on Hold,
Don't Pitch It—or Should You?

Sometimes the producer/manager/publisher will ask you not to pitch your song anywhere else until you hear from him. And if nothing else, it is an unspoken and unwritten rule that you will restrain from pitching the song for x amount of time.

This is all well and good—for them, but not for you! Let's analyze this situation in the hard, cold light of a very bright day. You have only so many songs and very few opportunities to pitch those songs. These "professionals" want you to hold off pitching your song to anyone else, based on a very vague implication that they might, may be, could be, possibly recording your song.

Analyzing this further, ask yourself a few questions: Whose career are you trying to build? Answer: *Yours*! What does the producer owe you? Answer: *Nothing*! Not even professional courtesy.

Now, your song has been on hold for 60 days. No word. No communication. And in that period, five other artists have come to your attention who would also be perfect for recording your song that is on hold. In the meantime you have passed up the chance to pitch your song elsewhere, because your song is on hold.

HOT TIP

Even if it's on hold, keep on pitching your song! That's right. Here's my reasoning.

▸ It is your career, not the producer's or the artist's; they already have careers.

▸ You have been asked to not do your job, which is to pitch your song and get it recorded.

▸ They are telling you, with nothing but a very vague promise (if that) that they are considering—maybe—recording your song, and to hold it for them.

Can you name any other business that works like this?

If you go to buy a car and need to think about it and you want to compare it with other cars, do you get to tell the salesman, "Hey, keep this car on hold for me for the next two weeks while I make up my mind"?

I think not!

The odds are that your song will not be recorded. The odds are that the producer will never tell you that he passed on your song. Being a good little songwriter, you didn't pitch your song anywhere else. You missed five other chances to have your song in the ear of a VIP. The key here is you. It is *your* song, *your* career. Look out for yourself.

The other side of that coin is this: if you get real lucky and get two recordings of your song at about the same time, are you doing something wrong? No more wrong than the producer who didn't tell you that they passed on your song. And many times, they don't notify you when the song is recorded … until they need the credits.

Here's my take and what I did in those types of cases. It only bit me twice over a 30-year period, and there were no consequences because I brought them a song they wanted to record.

The scenario: Your song is a single. The odds are that both recordings won't come out at the same time. That's good for you. The odds are that the VIPs involved won't ever know that some other VIP recorded the same song (the only time you don't do this is when you have signed a publishing deal with a publisher; then you don't pitch a published song to other publishers). If they do find out, you are innocent! You had no idea they were recording your song. You are in a win-win situation. Remember, it's your career. You now have your song recorded two times. You now have a real copyright. Once they pass on the song, meaning, they are not going to record it, they seldom bother to inform you that they will not be recording your song.

Only once have I had anything in writing from a producer guaranteeing and promising me that he would record my song. The producer, who was *on fire* at the time after several hits, told me he would not be going into the studio for one year. He wanted a hold for one year. He gave me a letter stating that he would record the song, and his intentions were that it would be a single. I agreed to the deal. One year later, they recorded the song and it was a single. Again, this happened only once in my 30-plus years in the music business.

I'm Not Going to Pitch My Songs to Those Guys—They'll Steal 'Em

I'm not going to go into copyright issues here, but let's look at this mostly unfounded fear. Ninety-nine point nine percent of the time, nobody will try to rip off your song as a whole; in other words, they won't steal your song, and then claim that they wrote it.

"I Love You." Wow, what a title! Do you have a clue how many songs have that title? Thousands! That's because you cannot copyright a title or the name of a song. What you copyright is the body of the song, the song as a whole.

Now if you truly have a unique title, then be a bit cautious about whom you tell the name of your song, such as a producer who is also a songwriter. However, it all depends on your relationship with that person. Every once in a while, you will read of a big lawsuit going on over a song that's been ripped off. With the thousands of songs written every month, a lawsuit only once in a while is a miracle.

Songwriters who are professionals and have been around for more than ten minutes need ideas. For instance, whenever some political event occurs and shakes up the world, songwriters come out of the woodwork with a song about it, and each one thinks that he or she is the only one to write about it. However, they don't sit where I have for more than 30 years. Whenever a writer would play me one of those "world ends" event songs, I would stop the CD, open a drawer and pull out a dozen songs of the same ilk. In part for the writer's education—there are other songwriters out there as well—you are not playing alone. It shows that other songwriters are thinking along the same lines, and that we are not always as unique as we like to think we are.

Ideas

Ideas are what get stolen or ripped off, and, in most cases, you will never have a clue that it's happening. For instance, you have written a pretty good song about "love's fire turning to ashes." Your song is just okay, and although it may be crafted well, it is just missing something. Ah-ha. *"Love's flame is as cold as ashes"* —is that a rip? Would you have thought of saying it like that? No, because that's not *exactly* what you wrote.

Were you ripped off? My answer here runs from "no comment" to "perhaps" to "blank." You fill in the space. What I do know is that you can't copyright an idea. If your song sparked an idea in somebody else's brain, that's what happens. An entire song being claim-jumped is very rare. Who heard your song? Or is it just that it is not a terribly original image?

On the other hand, rap has a rep for sampling, and has ended up losing millions of dollars in court because copyrighted songs were actually inserted into the rap recordings. In case you don't know, using any part of a song or any part of a recording without a license and written permission will land you in deep trouble. Record companies, music publishers, songwriters, and artists will approach you with an army of lawyers. Rap got its collective hands slapped by huge lawsuits, and rap lost.

Infringement of copyright is no joke.

The bottom line: Pitch your songs. You really can't tie yourself in knots over this minor problem. Being paranoid is not a good way to start your career. Pitch your songs.

CHAPTER **2 4**

You Pitched Your Song. Now What?

You've been trying to reach B. S. Producer or Ms. Publisher or whomever, and they haven't called you back. You left a message on Monday, no call back on Tuesday. You called again on Wednesday and left your message to please call back, and so on. Are you being ignored, feeling put off, or thinking that they don't like you? If you were paranoid, you would think that it could be all of the above.

Give these people the benefit of the doubt. I don't really like to, but to keep you sane, look at some of the following real possibilities:

HOT TIP

- They are really not in when you call. Really, how about that?
- They are in a meeting. Really?
- They are in the studio. Really?
- You are not a priority yet. Really?
- They don't feel like talking. Really?
- They didn't get your message. Really?
- They don't know how to tell you they are passing on your song. Really?
- They haven't listened to your song. Really?
- They are stalling you by not being professional. Really?
- They just can't take two minutes to say they haven't had a chance to listen to your song? Really?
- Really.

The key here is that you are not yet a priority to these people. When they are interested in your song, they will burn the wires getting back to you. They will answer your calls. Although I've been reminding you all along that it is your career, it is, for them, *their* career. These people, with all their trappings, are all wrapped up in themselves because they are in the "seat" and really *do* need great songs. None of these people have a career if they don't have great songs. Deep down, buried under all the ego, the truth lurks and the facts are that they need, want, crave, and will beg for a truly great song. Waiting in the wings are several hundred talented creative producers and publishers pushing and shoving to take their place. As long as you can understand that they really do need you and your great song, then you'll have a handle on the situation.

Back to being ignored: Just maybe, all their excuses are at least partially true. The most common truth is that they haven't listened yet. This can go on for weeks turning into months. Frustrating, to say the least.

Put yourself in that "big shot" chair for a minute so you'll be able to have an inkling of what these producers and publishers could be dealing with. This is where being a priority (or not) comes in.

If the producer or music publisher is hot, they might have anywhere from 50 to 200 packages and MP3 files piling up per week. It can be an overwhelming proposition. That equates to around 500 songs a month. They also have a business life, meetings, studio dates, and two-hour lunches to balance. Oh, and they have a home life as well. These professionals usually listen on a hit-and-miss basis.

I take CDs in my car and listen. What I like, I throw on the passenger side of the car; it's tough if I forget and someone is riding with me. What I pass on, I toss in the back seat. I also schedule a day of listening. I honestly listen to everything that comes to me—not the whole song all the way through, but enough to know if it's working and getting my attention.

I tell you this because I know that from 95 to 99 percent of producers and publishers don't have a clue about finding songs. If you ask them how they find songs, most will have the same stock answers: they might listen first to songs from writers or publishers they know. Or if someone, a lawyer, say, hyped a song or the writer to them.

Most people who should be listening for the next song that could make their career are always looking for excuses *not* to listen. Strange isn't it? But that is the reality.

Listening to all these songs is really hard work, and takes a huge amount of time. You have to have an ear that can take all the sound. Discerning that it's a bad demo but a good song is not easy. Listening can be an almost indescribable challenge. It can be hilarious, torturous, awful, wonderful, emotional, and "I found a great song!" all rolled into one. So give the artists, producers, and publishers the benefit of the doubt. They might have to make a decision, and that's hard for many of these folks to do. They might not ever listen to your song, but you could also get the phone call that will change your life and make your career.

You, calling B. S. Producer for the fourth time: *ring, ring* … "Hi, I'd like to speak to B. S. Producer. This is H. Songwriter." "Just a moment," a voice on the other end says, "I think he wants to talk with you." You don't have time to think because an instant later, B. S. is on the line. "Hey, hey, hey, man! Great to hear from you!" You're thinking, yeah, right, I've only called ten thousand times. "I want to talk to you about your song, 'Take a Hike, Mike, It's You I Like,'" he says. "Great melody, great lyric, just what I'm looking for, might even be the album title." You: "Uhhhh … okay." Him: "So when can you come in and we'll sign a contract?" You: "When can I come in?" You're thinking, I'm gonna get to see him. He wants me to pick the time. "Oh, how about 3 in the morning?" Him: "Fine! I can do that!"

See, it's just a matter of being a priority. When you *are* a priority, you *are* a *Priority* with a capital P. This might sound absurd, but it really isn't far from reality.

Some More on Pitching Songs

I've always felt that a real music publisher is a good editor. The songwriter pitches his or her song. The publisher listens and makes a few suggestions about words or lines, and with those changes, perhaps the publisher could work with the song.

This is a delicate procedure. Most publishers will not use this approach, and if they do, they are tentative about it. Often, the publisher is afraid of offending the writer. Perhaps he doesn't really know what is wrong with the song and his critique skills are lacking. Sometimes, a publisher is winging it, but an experienced publisher can usually spot the flaws in a song. A few of them can help you with a fix. Then they work the song. That's the old win-win situation.

The danger here is that some publishers will take advantage of the writer and add their name to the songwriting credit in order to secure a percentage of the song. (If I had done that with all the songwriters I've worked with and helped with line changes, my name would be all over the map.)

So how do you, the songwriter, respond to this? My suggestion is to try out what the publisher, or even a producer, has to say.

You can reject it or accept it, but don't be bullied. An honest, ethical publisher won't horn in on your song by demanding a writer's credit—and same deal with a producer or an artist.

Now, for the contradiction: there might be a time when it's just dumb not to share the copyright. There was a long-running late-night show for which the writer of the theme song shared the royalties with the star. This was the deal from the beginning. And this was a major songwriter. Was it a smart deal for him? You bet it was. He made big bucks for several decades.

Don't Get Mad or Argue

HOT TIP

It cannot be stated enough: If a proven producer or publisher (meaning, they have a track record) passes on your song, it's best not to argue with them. Don't get mad or try to talk them into signing your song. Either they hear it or they don't. You are not selling gizmos, so it's not a hard-sell item.

Step back after you leave the meeting and ask yourself a few questions:

▸ How much experience does this person have in the business?

▸ Are they a songwriter also?

▸ Do you know if they are?

- ▸ Do they have any kind of a track record?

- ▸ Did you check them out?

- ▸ Was it partly a personality problem? Or is it just you?

- ▸ Did you pitch the wrong type of song(s)?

- ▸ Did you do something to turn the publisher off?

- ▸ Be honest!

- ▸ About how old is he/she? (Contrary to what you might think, young is, many times, not so good.)

- ▸ Is this genre of music their expertise?

- ▸ Is it yours?

- ▸ What is their agenda?

- ▸ Did you do your homework?

- ▸ Is your song not really very good?

- ▸ What did they say to you about your song?

- ▸ Was it true?

- ▸ Be honest with yourself.

Any of these questions and more could lead to your answer. Here are a few of my experiences pitching songs:

I once was pitching a clever and sophisticated cheating song about a cheater being cheated on. I was very excited about this song. I played it for an A&R person (young). After it was over, he looked at me and said, "I don't get it." "Are you married?" I asked. "No," was his response.

I stood up, picked up my things and said, "I'll play it for you again about ten years after you are married." I left. This person didn't understand his own genre or his audience. No telling how many songs he missed out on.

Another time, I played a song for a producer who was on the rude side, beyond blunt! A real @%#&+!^. I played a couple of songs. Pass. Okay. I played a song that I knew was being recorded as we sat in the meeting. The song I was pitching to this producer for his artist was already being recorded by a similar type of artist. The producer in all his wisdom declared I would never get that song recorded. "Really?" said I. "That's funny," I thought. I don't recall the exact words that were exchanged but "stupid," "jerk," and "idiot" remained in my brain. In my mind I jumped up on this guy's desk and ran him out of the room. Dreaming, I left. The best revenge is to wait it out, then come back with different songs or better songs. Get one cut! Don't get mad; get even!

Pitching Songs You Don't Like

"I have to really believe in a song and really like/love it before I pitch it!" How many times have you heard this statement? I've heard it hundreds of times. I don't agree at all. Not one little bit. I think it's the sign of an amateur lacking talent, or of someone not very smart and who most definitely is not a professional.

You Don't Have to Like a Song to Pitch It

"I really have to love a song to work it and keep pitching the song. Otherwise I just can't deal with it" or "I have to be honest with myself and believe in a song to work with it."

Nonsense, all you need is to understand it. Understand it and know who the song's audience would be. As in "I don't really like this song, but it's exactly what Teenage Idol Guy is doing and he would be perfect for this song." Or, "It's right on the money for Miss Golden Pipes."

HOT TIP

Understanding Your Market

▸ Break down the market into artists.

▸ Examine the kind of songs they like.

▸ It's not about what you like.

▸ You are just the messenger that brings the song.

The song is just a bag of hot air. It is a package that you, the writer and song plugger, is placing in the ear of the listener. If I waited for only the songs I loved and believed in, I wouldn't have had many songs recorded. This is a business. Understand and study what the business uses. Use the business of pitching songs that work for that artist.

I have pitched and worked with many songs I didn't like. Sometimes it was an assignment, or I just understood why that song worked for a specific artist.

Speaking of songs you believe in, I'll bet if you listen to a hit writer's catalogue or crack open the vault of a music publisher, they will all have more than a few songs that will stun you when you realize that they have never been recorded. These are songs that were, and are, believed in. Why is this? No one knows. They will all play you some songs that have been buried in albums that should have been a single. Those songs are waiting to be found by an astute producer and a smart artist. (Yes, those combinations are rare.)

I'm one of those music publishers. I have a few songs that are killer and have never been recorded. I pitched them like crazy—"Nope, can't use it." I have published and have some recordings of album cuts that are waiting to be picked up as singles. I continue to pitch them. Why aren't they cut? Timing. Relationships. The unknown.

There are only so many songs that can be cut. Politics enter the room. (The producer writes his song, and they are recording that song; the producer's girlfriend wrote the next song; the producer's buddies wrote the next three songs; the artist wrote one; and a hundred other reasons.) Break down that door; it can be done. You just have to keep pitching your songs.

CHAPTER **26**

International
Song Plugging

The U.K. is a good place to start (they speak a form of English there). They have trade publications. France, Spain, the Benelux countries (Belgium, the Netherlands, Luxembourg), Germany, Mexico, Japan, Taiwan, China, Brazil, and so on, all have trade publications to which you can subscribe and feature artists about whom you can learn and track down to pitch your songs.

You have at least 36 countries that could potentially bring you a tidy sum. You can look into cowriting with a writer in another country. The Internet and songwriter forums have opened doors even wider to international songwriting collaboration. It's your job to take advantage of those tools. Keep the same logs and contacts as you would if they lived in your city.

You have to apply yourself to the subtle styles in other countries and learn what is working there. By doing your homework, you could be up to speed very quickly.

HOT TIP

- ▸ International song plugging on the songwriter level is just blooming.

- ▸ It is not impossible; as a matter of fact it is pretty easy to do.

- ▸ The international market is waiting for you and your songs.

Fan Clubs and Professional Organizations

Many of you monitor YouTube and Facebook and check out online fan sites and magazines. You might even pick up a tip or a contact once in a while. Remember that these are all just big PR sites and seldom contain anything you as a writer can use.

Fan clubs fall into the same category: they are not in the business of giving any kind of information that would be helpful to a songwriter. However, if you are good at reading between the lines, you might find out if a particular artist will be touring near you, or even where he or she might be staying.

BMI, ASCAP, and SESAC

You know who they are. You know what they do, and many other books cover this area very well. But did you know that they have writer/publisher reps? Yes, they do. It is now part of your job to get these names and meet those reps; they are not hard to find.

If you are a member of ASCAP, BMI, or SESAC at this time, that's good. The reps are there to help you and listen to your songs. If they like you and your songs, they will set up contacts for you or pass your song along to some producers, artists, managers, or publishers. If you do not belong yet, a rep will try to encourage you to join or think about joining their respective organization.

The reps can be a big help. Reps from these societies have helped me all throughout my career. You want to impress them with a few knock-the-walls-down songs. If you can get their attention, they can help open doors for you.

Songwriting Organizations Can Be Helpful

Many times, these organizations have guest speakers from different areas of the industry. They are there for you to bounce songs off of and to offer industry information. They can give you opportunities to meet and work with cowriters. Sometimes they offer services like demo recording rates and song-plugging services. Producers and publishers/song pluggers are the most frequent guests. Some of these "pros" will be better speakers than others. Some will be able to express the "why" and the "why not" of a song in explicit terms; others may stumble all over themselves verbally, but have the ability to pick out a great song. Pay attention and take notes when these folks show up to speak to your group. If you learn only one new thing, you are ahead of the game.

Attend those seminars, no matter who the speaker is. No matter the level of the pro, pay attention to what is said. You will also meet other writers. You can only help your own career, and that is what it is about. It is your career. The bottom line is that belonging to an organization is just one more tool for you to use to get ahead.

Song-Plugging Services

Be careful. Beware. Investigate the service. Ask for proof of the songs they have gotten recorded. Ask for references and then follow up on them. Ask how many clients they represent and figure out how many songs that adds up to. You can pay attention to and pitch only so many songs at a time. How much is the cost? If they get the song cut, do they share in the publishing, or any percentage of the income, and for how long? What makes them so hot? How many of your songs are they willing to rep?

Try This

Pitch the song-plugging service a few songs that are representative of your writing. Play them a few of your best. Then throw in two "ringers" that are just crap. Ask for an evaluation of the four or five songs. If the service likes them all and breaks them down for you, you just might have a problem.

Are there good, honest plugging companies? Most likely, but I'm very wary of these outfits. I will most likely receive some flack about this, but I stand by my experience; yours may be very positive.

Exception to the Rule

An exception to the rule is TAXI, which functions as a large A&R company that pitches to major and independent record companies at the request of the record company, the artist, the publisher, or the producer. (I am a consultant to TAXI.) While using TAXI isn't cheap, you will get a real shot at having your song heard by a major producer, artist, or publisher if it makes the grade. And you can have your song evaluated by a professional in the music business. Your ability to get in the door from long distance is also increased. Think of TAXI as another avenue you can take to advance your career.

Song Contests

The one that wins at this game is the organization putting on the contest. As far as I'm concerned, contests just separate the writer from a few bucks. They all make promises of having certain big-time judges and having your songs exposed to artists and publishers and producers. You might get lucky. But for the most part, I would pass.

However, on the flip side, always look at who is putting on the contest. Once in a while, they can be worthwhile, and by that I mean you could win some money or gear. Everything else they have to say is generally hype. Investigate. This doesn't mean that some song contest won't come along in the future and be the place to enter your songs.

Songwriter Forums on the Net

I've looked in on many of these forums and blogs and even joined in some of the discussions, offering some small bits of advice. My findings are that most of the information they offer is fairly solid. Knowledgeable people participate and are willing to share what they know, or what their experience has been.

Conversely, I have also seen things that are dead wrong or only *almost* right. I've seen scams uncovered so fast it would make your head swim. That's a good thing, and it is a learning curve for all who read and need the correct information.

The amount of information that is offered by some of these songwriter forums is almost overwhelming if you are a newbie, but it gives you a starting place to ask questions and hopefully get an answer that is correct. If the answer is not right-on, there seems to be no lack of folks chiming in and stating otherwise. Many of these forums have professional members, some act as mentors, and they offer up advice as needed.

CHAPTER **28**

The Session Players

When making demos, don't be put off by what the musicians in the studio have to say about your songs. They are not record consumers for the most part, and their opinions are mostly based on if they like the chord structure and the mood. That statement may sound a bit strong, but players seldom pick out the hits. Their collective heads are about making the record with their talent as players, not as experts on hit songs. Many times they are into certain cool, artsy chord changes, and transitions that only a few people ever hear. Their job is to participate in making the demo and showcasing your song, making a diamond from coal.

A note is in order here. Copyright law is in a state of flux and interpretation, and lawsuits can fly all over some songs at the drop of a chord. Therefore, I feel it is my duty to inform you of a few things that should be done to safeguard your copyright. Whenever you are recording a demo of your song(s), for each and every song, you should get completed release and work-for-hire forms from each of the demo players, stating that they have no copyright interest in the song. As a "work-for-hire" player, all they can legally claim is the "one-time" pay for the session. The same goes for the engineer. *Sign here!* I am not a lawyer and I cannot give you legal advice, but I can provide legal information that is logical information. You can get this info and a simple letter agreement from any entertainment attorney. (See the Appendices at the end of this book for other recommended books.)

What Else Do You Need to Know?

CHAPTER 29

Alternative Ways Your Songs Can Make Money

I Want My Songs on TV and in the Movies

HOT TIP

How does one work these pitches? Again, the trades are your friends. In the case of movies and television, you need to read the *Hollywood Reporter* and *Daily Variety*. They are published every day. Once a week the Hollywood Reporter lists the TV and film productions that are going on, with the telephone numbers and other information. The phone numbers are your key.

Cold calling is always hard to do, but it's part of the game. Call and ask for the producer, or for the music coordinator's or music supervisor's number. Also ask the person who answers the phone if they know whether the producer is looking for original songs for the movie or show. Sometimes they won't know, but sometimes they will put you through to the producer's office. Sometimes they will put you through to the music coordinator or supervisor. Sometimes they haven't even thought about music yet—music comes at the very end of a film or TV production. Sometimes they will tell you to call back.

In all of these instances, you break out your phone file and begin your "File." Right now.

You might make 20 calls and get nowhere at all. That's today. Next Thursday, the first call you may hear could be, "Hey, I need a song about a 'jukebox that lives in the Rock 'n' Roll Hall of Fame!' I need it last week, what do you have for me?" Or, "I need a 'pedestal' love song, a power ballad to go over the end credits—get it to me in one week!" Cool.

By reading the trades every day, you will begin to pick up more information about movies and TV shows, who is involved in making them, and who is handling the music. Then it really isn't hard to track down those companies or individuals.

One thing you should know is this: many movie and television people on the production side don't know jack about music. For the most part, they give it a low place on the totem pole of production value, and they are cheap about it. Again, they don't have a clue about good songs or bad songs or so-so songs or real junk. It's the music supervisors, especially with television, who really have the influence and have convinced the production people that showcasing cutting-edge artists and bands in the soundtracks can be a plus.

Pitching songs to movie and television people is a maddening process, but it can pay off big! For instance, I made a deal for an original song in a low-budget movie. The licensing was well under a thousand dollars. The song had three writers, and after all the splits, there was no real money; it just covered my phone bill. The writers were not happy with me. When the movie came out, I had to see it three times before I could ID and hear about 15 seconds of the song.

Now comes the luck of the draw, just because we went for it: the movie was a blockbuster hit, so much so that the movie studio, in all its wisdom, decided to release a soundtrack album. The song was included on the album, and went on a roller coaster ride zooming up the charts, to the tune of over 12 million album sales. Now, that's a nice tune to hear. You just never know what is going to happen in this business.

Unions, Trade Organizations, and Guilds

Unions have memberships. Unions have membership meetings. Unions vote on issues. Unions go on strike, or threaten to. Opportunity is knocking for the thinking songwriter.

I have a friend who took advantage of a union. After meeting with the local union heads and then the planning committee, he and the union hammered out a songwriting deal for coming up with songs containing the union's messages. My friend wrote several songs for the union, using the theme that the union bosses were pushing to the membership. The studio time was paid for up front by the union. The songs were paid for on delivery. It was a one-time fee.

This writer-singer retained the ownership of the copyrights and, over a four-year period, made more money than many writers ever make in their whole careers. In addition, this writer-singer was paid to travel and perform live in front of an audience of about ten thousand union leaders (a good potential fan base), and was compensated handsomely for the live appearance.

Sure, the songs were not high songwriting art that were meant to be classics, but the writer delivered the goods and the union heads and the members loved them. Some of these songs were 45 seconds long, or one minute to two minutes, max.

Ask yourself: Are you are a pro? Can you deliver?

Politics—City, County, State, and the Nation

I have a songwriter friend who hooked up with a political party and was paid to write "Vote for Me," "Look at Me" types of songs that covered an entire state. For delivering the goods, this writer did very well on payday. You can explore this avenue by making phone calls, attending political meetings where you live, and making a pitch about your ideas right on the spot.

Another writer I know wrote an antidrug song and submitted an idea to go with it about grade school kids not doing drugs. For every class where it was played, he was paid good bucks. The writer created a program that was expanded throughout the state school system. It is ongoing. Look into this kind of opportunity where you live.

How about this one? A writer was at a bank and was talking with one of its vice presidents, who mentioned that the bank was looking for a premium as a giveaway gift for new accounts. It was going to be pushed from Thanksgiving to New Year's. The writer-singer suggested that a Christmas album with some new songs about Christmas might be a good premium gift. The bank went for it and the writer-singer did very well, indeed. How many banks are close to where you live in your city? You can make an appointment today.

Another writer was having a bit of success, but nothing earthshaking. Frustrated at the pace and feeling things could be better, the writer wrote a Christmas song and, subsequently, it was recorded by a major artist for a Christmas album. The sales were very good, as they often are with Christmas albums. Happy holidays! An idea was born. Specialize in Christmas songs. Well, this had been done before, but he had a different slant on an old idea.

The writer started a campaign to find out who was going to be recording Christmas albums. Many of these albums are recorded as early as March, April, May, and June. So your holiday hat has to be on early.

As is often the case, this writer could produce only so many above-average Christmas songs. After thinking it through, the songwriter went to some songwriting friends and told them what he needed. Going from songwriter to music publisher to song plugger is an easy transition for some people. Our songwriter-publisher reached out to the local songwriter community and soon was representing several dozen songs—and getting them recorded. From this startup came the idea of all the holiday songs that could be recorded—for Easter, Valentine's Day, birthdays, Thanksgiving, Mothers Day, Father's Day, and so on.

This holiday songwriter-publisher is a very smart, hardworking person and works the catalogue all year long. A career is born. A niche is filled.

Children's Songs—the Kids' Market

At one time, the children's market was almost totally sewn up, controlled by a few large companies. It was nearly impossible to break into these companies, no matter how good you were. Good news: that market has changed dramatically for the better. Better for you, the songwriter, and for the consumer.

The children's, tween, and teen marketplace is bigger than huge. The possibilities for marketing are endless. If you have the knack for writing and promoting, you have this wide-open market waiting just for you.

Clever characters in a song, coupled with great stories, voices, and illustrations, are bait that attracts people to products (known as parent traps) they buy for their kids. This special area of the business can be extremely lucrative. A little investigation should arm you with enough information to see if this niche of the music business is for you.

Composing children's songs can be a challenge to the best of writers. Writing songs for the one-digit age group entails walking a fine line between what-is-understood-by-the-kids and what they perceive as funny. You as the adult may think that six-year-old Mikey will "get it." Don't count on it. As with any genre within a genre, I urge you to study the history of kids' songs and immerse yourself in the music, including what is happening right now.

Kid tunes could be your future as a songwriter. This could prove to be a solid move for you. You may never be known well, even among other professional writers, but your bank account will just chuckle at that news.

As far as pitching your kid tunes, there are many companies. They have creative directors and producers, just like the rest of the biz. The bigger media companies are places to start. You may have to develop your demo pitch on a more elaborate plate before you make your presentation.

Getting an appointment with anyone can be very difficult in the kid market. Make sure that your product is protected on all fronts of copyright—that is, its characters, its music, its art.

Grab your kid muse and play the way you did as a youngster. *It's your career.* Get to work.

Commercials, Ringtones, and New Media

There are other alternative ways for you to write songs. Commercials are a very difficult market to break into. You have to look around and *see songwriting wherever you look.* It may not be exactly where you want to go. It is just a way to make some money and write songs. This gives you experience. And not only do you gain experience, you are forced by time constraints to write hooks and a good melody that fit into a 30- to 60-second slot.

Consider cell phones. Ringtones. You are using your phone every day and someone is writing those ring tones, so why not you? "Mobisodes," the studios' cell phone delivery of short episodes, use songs, or what I call snippets of a song—one or two lines.

How about music or songs for videogames? The video market is exploding for the savvy songwriter. Professional writers often are given "project" songs to write. Writing on demand separates the professional from the wannabe. Look at it as part of your growth and training as a songwriter.

These are examples of the various niche markets available to songwriters. Check out every possibility that requires music. You might like them, and the bucks they bring in could add up to a very good year.

Christian Music

The Christian-music market is huge. It is as hard to crack as any commercial market because *it is* a commercial market; believe me—it is commercial.

Although Christian music is a whole entity unto itself, you should study this market just like the other markets. It has its own trades and stars and charts. Some people are more comfortable working in this market because they feel they have a connection through their own beliefs. If you feel that is the case, then you have the niche that many writers look for. Working in this area of the music biz takes the same amount of energy and conviction and hard work as the secular market does.

New-Age Music

This is another niche market that has its own distinct sound and message. New-age music has its own market, and a lot of people love it. It, too, has its own charts and trades, conventions, and alternative media coverage. If this is your market, all the rules and tips in this book work here as well.

Writing for Hire

In many of the niche markets just mentioned, you may encounter a work-for-hire situation. Here's what that may entail:

1. You don't participate in the ownership of the copyright.

2. Your name may or may not be credited.

3. You will never make any additional monies or royalties on this song.

4. Many people will never believe you ever wrote the song!

Here is the upside:

1. You might make a nice chunk of cash. Sometimes, more than you would have otherwise.

2. You made a good contact and an impression. That could lead to more work.

3. Who cares if no one believes you?

4. I "ghost-produced" for a few folks, and you wouldn't believe me if I told you who!

5. I co-wrote songs with no credit but got paid.

6. Some writers have spent entire careers writing for hire, and have done well for themselves.

7. Writing songs for commercials often falls into this category.

It's songwriting and it takes a special talent to write a hit song for a commercial. Don't pass up an opportunity to write a commercial. Writing in tight formats and constricted time frames is a real talent.

The "L" Word: Lawyers

Yucky yuck! Contracts—*uggghhh*. Let's look at this a little bit. Other books have covered this area pretty well and lawyers have written books about the music business. I'm covering it a little differently in a page.

Don't Skip This Part!

Lawyers: some of my best friends are *not* lawyers. I have dealt with lawyers over the years because if you are in this business, at some point you will have to work with them. They can help you, even protect you, but at a price. Sometimes it's worth it. Sometimes not! Lawyers are good at taking your money. Any dealings you may have with them should be in writing. What exactly are they going to do? Know exactly what their fee is and what they are providing you in return. This is a key point, as in, *really* important. If they do not want to commit in writing, just a memo or email (print it and save it) to you will suffice. If they won't do that, then seek other counsel.

Lawyers can make or break a deal. Many of them push too far for too much for no reason other than their own ego.

In spite of my aversion to this bunch (I am speaking in very broad terms—I do have friends who are lawyers, but I pretend they are not lawyers), at times you will have to hire one. This is key. The lawyer is working for you. *Remember that*! Keep it that way. You can also fire them! That is good to remember. The lawyer is hired by you, so don't let them take that away from you. *You* are in control. So tell him or her what you want. The lawyer's job is to put what the deal is into legal jargon of the biz. That's it. That's all. Simple. *It's your career.*

Songwriter Publishing Contracts

If you are dealing with a straight-up publisher, his or her contract should be okay. Maybe. You can always try to get a reversion clause if the song is not recorded within a certain time frame. Give them at least two years. If you have done your homework, you can usually tell if the contract is okay. If you can't determine whether the contract is okay to sign, find an entertainment attorney. Pay attention to what your lawyer says. Keep a copy of your signed contract, and use it as a model for other song deals—it's just a very simple song contract. After the fact, no one wants to hear, "I'm an artist, I don't understand." Understand it! Take a course! Go to school. Get it right. Understanding a simple single song contract is part of it. Understand what you are signing. Do not trust *anyone* who offers you a contract. Best to have it checked out. Read every word of your contract and ask questions until you understand it. Don't worry about sounding stupid. You are being smart by asking and getting answers.

I can't tell you how many times over the years some writer brought me a contract that he or she had signed years ago, and said, "I didn't really understand what I was signing." Right—I'm not a lawyer and I can't give legal advice. But I do know BS when I see it. My answer is usually something like, "What the hell is wrong with you? Can't you read and think?!" And I say it loud! I'm sure all of you get the message.

It's All About Pitching Your Songs!

What's the sense of learning how to pitch and getting your song recorded if you don't reap the benefits? A small digression is necessary here. When a music publisher publishes your song, that means he or she believes in your song and wants to work with your song. Meaning, the music publisher wants to pitch it! The music publisher thinks that he or she can get an artist to record your song. This is what you want.

So, what to do? Sit back and wait for the good news, knowing the publisher will get you a recording? Don't count on it. You aren't helpless, baby! Relating to mechanicals, the song and the copyright are now a fifty-fifty proposition, meaning for every one hundred bucks that comes in, you each get fifty.

All right, but first the recording. You have every right—legally, morally, and ethically—to keep right on pitching your song; you just cannot pitch to other music publishers. You can pitch to producers, artists, managers, A&R, agents, and friends. Why not increase your odds of having the song recorded? Just maybe, you are better (or luckier) than the publisher at pitching songs.

You say, "That's the publisher's job." I say, that's true, and he or she will pitch your song. However, what if you run into Ms. Golden Pipes and you have an opportunity to hand her your song? Of course you'll do it!

I've published a few songs the writer got recorded and have always given him or her credit for it. In this biz, everyone takes credit for the song. So what! You can laugh all the way to the bank.

Keep Pitching

Don't rest after you place your song with the publisher. Keep pitching. Give the publisher your ideas about whom he or she could pitch to. Then, try to get the song to some additional contacts yourself. It's a team effort and the more meetings there are, the greater your chances are of getting a recording. What gets turned down today, the producer may love next week. Here's a news flash for you. Most publishers will be hot for your ditty and will pitch it. They will pitch once, twice, three times, maybe even six or seven times. Then, they don't get any holds and only negative feedback. In the meantime, they've signed three more songs from another writer, plus two of his staff writers have come up with a couple of smokin' songs. This is the way it works.

I once pitched a song 105 before it was cut—by a major act. I was a little nuttier than most publishers. I *knew* the song *worked*. Many publishers won't do that; even if they really like the song, they don't have the luxury or the time frame to keep pitching that song over others in the catalog. They have to move on. That's the reality. Another part of the reality is that publishers tend to second-guess their own belief in a song and lose any loyalty to a song very quickly when they don't get positive feedback.

Now if the publisher does get a cut placed, great! The whole process worked. That's the way it's supposed to be. You should try to help the process along whenever and wherever you can. *It's your career!*

Seminars About the Biz

Be sure to go to seminars about the music business, even if you don't think they will be that interesting. Endure the boring parts and the stuff you already know. If you pick up just one bit of information that you didn't know, tuck that in your collection of "how to do that." Then, you're one step further along in your career.

Learn all you can about the ins and outs of the business, and how it works. You have every reason to arm yourself with information on copyright and the process of how you get paid and by whom. Hearing some of the stories these pros can tell is a lesson for you.

I once worked with a hit group who had racked up an impressive run of hit songs. They did very well for themselves as artists and writers, but they didn't understand the basics of getting paid for their copyrights. Oh, sure, they got the checks, but they just didn't *get* it. Once, I sat in a meeting with this group, their producer, and their manager. They asked me to explain to them the difference between *mechanical* and *performance* incomes, and who paid them that money! This, after having a string of hits! Furthermore, it had been explained to them before. Your job is to understand the business. It really isn't complicated.

There is a chance that you, as a writer, will become an artist. Know how your business works for everything, including synchronization, performance, international and domestic licensing deals, and so on. *It is your career.*

Co-Writing

There's an old saying that when you co-write, you should write with someone who you think is a better writer than you are. If you have a writing partner, you have potentially doubled your song-pitching abilities and opportunities. I hope that your partners work as hard as you do at plugging your song, as well. Stay in contact with your co-writers and compare notes about pitches. Establish that you control your 50 percent of the song (or whatever your agreed-upon percentage is). Put it in writing. This is very important for the future of your shared copyright. See Chapter 30, "The 'L' Word: Lawyers."

When two of you write a song, you both have ownership of the song and its copyright. Meaning, for example, if you wrote the song alone, you would own 100 percent of the song and control 100 percent of it. When you co-write and the split is 50-50, you each control 50 percent of the song.

You can submit or pitch the song to a publisher who can sign the song (publish the song). The publisher then owns and controls 100 percent of the song and the publishing rights. The two writers retain the writer's share as 50-50 writing partners. The breakdown is this: for every $100 of income, not counting "performance" income, the publisher gets $50 and each writer gets $25, splitting the $50 between the two writers. For example, if you wrote the song by yourself, then the above income flow would be $50 for the publisher and $50 for the writer.

Should you write with two other writers, making a total of three writers, then, you would split the writers' share in thirds. However, you don't always have to split evenly! It can get more complex, if, for instance, another writer contributed a few meaningful words or notes and should be recognized and rewarded for this effort. You agree on 15 percent. At the same time, another writer also was in the room and made suggestions as you composed the song, so you award her contribution with a 10 percent share.

You each control your shares. Each of you can sign with a different publisher, but that publisher can only own and represent the same share you do as the writer. However, if all of you go to the same publisher, then that publisher represents all of you. The publisher's share is 100 percent of the publishing, and the breakdown for the writers in the above example is 75 percent, 15 percent, and 10 percent, respectively. This will apply for all income streams for the writers.

It is important that you agree with the other writers and you have an agreement, *in writing*, on your percentage breakdowns.

I'm Saving This Song for Myself

Really? Good for you! My next question is "*Why* are you saving *this* song? Are you being pitched as an artist? Great! In most cases, that's one pitch at a time to the record companies, one chance as an artist. You are looking at a time frame of up to one year to get an answer. If you were to pitch this great song that you've been saving for yourself, you would have innumerable chances of the song being recorded. I'm not saying your artist deal can't happen. It does happen. Artist deals have been known to come out of recognition of a good tune that he or she wrote. At any given time, several hundred artists are being pitched to the record labels. However, your song can go to 30 artists who have deals, and that's just this week! And that can only help to give you more stature, and get you more respect as a writer. Do you think this is the last great song you are going to write? It's your call and it's your career. You are a songwriter first, last, and always, so pitch your songs.

I Don't Think My Songs Are Good Enough

Maybe, maybe not! In life, you have to take some chances. Perhaps you are the lone wolf in town and you don't know any other writers. Or, you don't want to play your songs for family or friends. You are a closet writer, and the world will never know if you don't step out and see what kind of reaction you get to your songs.

If you just write lyrics, you have to hook up with a composer. If you only write music, then you need that lyricist. Some of the best songs in history came from teams. If you are a songwriting team, every tip in this book can be doubled.

In order to find out about your songs, you may need to join a songwriting organization. Such organizations are found in almost every state in the USA and in many of the larger cities. Colleges have programs, as well. Depending on the organization, you can get some feedback from other writers. At least you are exposing your work to other people who are in the same boat as you are.

Many times, these organizations have professional guest speakers, and some of them will listen to songs and critique them. This is a good way to learn. I have been a guest speaker many times with these songwriter organizations and have seen first-hand what good talent is out there.

HOT TIP

One of the great things about being a songwriter is that you can do it at any age.

That's cool.

24 Hours a Day, Seven Days a Week

The music business never stops. Writing, making contacts, recording demos, co-writing, pitching, making copies, MP3s, and CDs, writing letters, e-mailing, printing labels, listening to artists and all the other work involved, taking care of yourself and your home and family, and, in most cases, holding down a full-time job because you are not yet a full-time writer making the big bucks, takes up time and requires substantial stamina and organization.

The music business is a tough, time-consuming, giant taskmaster. It can and will use you, tease you, deceive you, be wonderful to you, choose you as a talent, beat you up, take your money, and provide more money and perks than one person could hope for.

After a while, its ups and downs, its negatives, may get you down.

What to do? Back off. Take a weekend and go away. Don't write. Go camping, go to the beach, to the mountains, to a theme park—just get away from it. Do this at least a few times every month or so. It will refresh you, revitalize you, and give you some new ideas. Most importantly, you won't be a burnout. You pay yourself first with other parts of your life.

One "up" day can carry you through a month of low days. This business is a turndown business, and it can get to you. What to do? Get a hobby. Spend time with loved ones and friends. Have friends who are not in the business. You get the picture. Be good to yourself.

CHAPTER 36

They Killed My Recording

In a seminar or a songwriting class or in any group of music people, when the talk turns to getting songs recorded, with all the street talk and myths about the process, I usually offer some advice I have given for years, driven by real-life experience.

One of my favorite excuses I've heard used to explain why a record has disappeared is this one: "They put it on the shelf." "They killed the record." Right! What that means is the folks at the record company, somewhere after the fact of recording this artist, made a decision that perhaps they made a mistake. They did not hear a hit song or even a song that might get some attention. Or, the artist or the manager got a highly placed person in the company really steamed. Or, the artist wasn't living up to the expectations of the record company, or any other reasons you can dredge up. Reality is often chilling. Most of the time, the record company decides to cut its losses right then and there and shelve the record. That's all there is to it.

You cannot force the public to buy an artist or a song. No matter what the marketing is—if the public doesn't like the song, they won't buy your record. Even if they are fans of the artist, sales will be off if the song doesn't kick ass, or work, or isn't right for the artist.

Once, I got in a bind with a single recorded by a major group and produced by a hot producer. Just as the song was released, the group's renegotiations with the record label fell apart. My copyright had been reviewed in *Billboard* and the other trades. It was getting some major airplay.

As the group walked away from the record label, my single crashed like a lead balloon. The label pulled the plug on any promotion. That was just bad luck, bad timing, and miserable. No one can anticipate an action like this that kills a record. Don't interpret this as being "put on the shelf"; it isn't really.

Many albums have been put on the shelf because no promo person could get behind promoting even one song on the album. The promo folks just didn't hear it. No one at the label would back it up, so it died. Are they right? Sometimes yes, sometimes no.

I recall becoming aware of a song by a group that we represented. The album had been around our offices for four or five months. We really weren't into it very much. However, some little voice whispered, "Listen again. I think there's a hit song." Yep, there was. On the next listen, we found it buried in the album that previously put us to sleep. The song went to No. 1 on the charts. By chance, things happen in your favor, as well as against. It is a roller coaster. Take a ride.

Who Is the Artist? Who Is the Producer?

You find out about an artist who is looking for material. You have never heard of the artist. This singer has never had a record deal before. Like most, you are a bit less than enthusiastic about pitching your hit songs.

Find out what you can about the artist—style, types of material, voice, looks, and so on. Many times, you can get a lot of information straight from the producer, a secretary, or an assistant.

You have gathered as much info as you could about the new artist. It's time to turn to the producer. Who is the producer? Who has he or she already produced? Was he or she successful? Has he or she produced more than one act?

By being successful with more than one act, I mean exactly that. You should be aware that many producers have only had a one-winner act. One of the producers I know produced an act and several albums that sold Gold and Platinum each time out of the box. But this producer also produced many, many other acts that failed to do a thing.

HOT TIP

Be aware that the most celebrated and successful producers usually have more failures than successes!

Read that sentence again.

Conversely, in the case of the unknown artist and a relatively known producer, the producer is the person on whom you want to focus. Listen to his or her past records and songs. If you can talk with the producer, try to see what music he or she is really looking for. Sometimes, getting this information is almost impossible. Be gently persistent. Remember that in this case, the producer is the star, as is the situation a great deal of the time.

A real producer's job is to perpetuate and enhance the artist's career with absolutely great songs, no matter where they come from. That's your job. You are the wordsmith, so dazzle them with your great song. It's your career.

Giving Up Too Soon on Your Song

Almost all writers are guilty of giving up too soon on their songs. I know for a fact that publishers are certainly guilty of it.

What do I mean by "giving up too soon"? If you follow some of my suggestions, you will keep a file of the contacts you have pitched to and when. If you keep a cross-file with the name of your song and whom you've pitched it to, you will know exactly how many times your song was pitched.

I've found that most writers pitch the same song no more than 20 times, and that's on the high side. In fact, most writers pitch the same song less than ten times, many only about five times, and then they move on to the next song. Why?

So, the writer pitches the song. The publisher turns it down. A producer turns it down. Two more publishers turn it down. This process has taken, perhaps, five weeks. In the meantime, our writer has two brand-new songs she wants to pitch.

The first song is shoved to one side. She thinks the two new songs are better. The first song is hung out to dry. Onto the newer, "better" songs. The cycle continues.

Music publishers sometimes have only one artist in mind for a song. They pitch it once and move on to the next song and artist. This happens a lot more than you might think. In most cases, they may pitch a song only five or six times over the course of a year. Why is this?

The music publisher has many songs to choose from and a lot of contacts to pitch to. Our music publisher pitches this hot new tune to the one artist he has in mind. Then he gets a pass. Okay, so this tune isn't great. Move on.

Then this happens to you:

> Songwriter: "Hey, did you pitch my song lately?"
>
> Music Publisher: "Yeah, we got passed on."
>
> Songwriter: "So who do you have in mind now?"
>
> Music Publisher: "I'm working on that; I've got a few ideas."

In the worst-case scenario, no, he probably doesn't! Other songs have his attention now. Sometimes a publisher will stay behind a song and pitch it several more times. However, *you* can continue to pitch the song.

How to stop this cycle? First, make a list of the song titles you have written that you feel are professional songs and are in the competition. You have a list of 30 songs on your "most-commercial" song list. You have a list of ten songs in your "off-the-wall" song list.

As you discover artists who are looking for material, go down your list of songs and match up (cast) a few to these artists. Next, with these artists in mind, play your song. Aha! That's perfect for Hit Artist Number 1. Or, nope, that won't really work. No matter how well you know the song, play it again with each and every artist in mind. With this method, your songs always have a chance. It's easy to forget that a certain song sounds great for a specific artist. The opposite may be true as well; after you play it again with that particular artist in mind, it may not really fit. Remember, if a song really is wrong for the artist, it can be just as smart not to pitch it.

HOT TIP

If you have ten songs you feel are great, you can keep pitching them for years—20 times, 50 times, 100 times. Common sense will tell you that this list will change a bit over time as you write better songs, but some of the songs will remain strong even with the distance of time and objectivity.

I pitched a song 105 times before a major act cut it. I worked another song for about four months and pitched it about 35 times. Not only did it get recorded, but it also went to No. 1.

The Good Publisher

As a writer, you may think that you really know your song in an intimate way—no one else may understand it. Maybe. Maybe not. That depends on the relationship that you (and your song) have with your music publisher.

Your publisher may have a point of view about your song, your baby, that perhaps you have never heard before. A good publisher who works your song, who hustles as a publisher, should and does know your song extremely well, but in a different light.

The good publisher will come to understand why your baby is so precious and deserving of all the attention and money it takes to get a song recorded. A good publisher really cares about your songs, and it becomes a personal challenge to try hard as hell to get that song recorded. A good publisher will have listened to your song many more times than you have.

Your good publisher will be on such an intimate basis with your song that he or she will know it backwards and forwards. Your good publisher may pitch your song to artists you never considered.

By the same token, if you have an idea about an artist who might be a good candidate for your song, tell your publisher—no one thinks of everything. A good music publisher becomes attached to your song and it becomes his or her song. It really is her or his song as much as it is yours. The good music publisher ends up working with the song in ways that go beyond just listening to it: burning copies, talking up and hyping the song over breakfasts, lunches, cocktails, and dinners. She may take the song along just to play it for friends, or other publishers, or to play it in the "off pitch" for producers and artists, risking being turned down, turned off, and sometimes trashed. Or, she may encounter the "Oh my god" reaction of "This is perfect, fantastic, just what I'm looking for."

Your good publisher suffers through all the emotional ups and downs on a face-to-face or phone-to-ear basis of "Yes," "No," "I love it," "What the hell were you thinking?" "Close, but no cigar," or "I'm recording this song right now!" This is what a publisher lives for.

Your good publisher loves your song as much as you do. Sometimes your good publisher will care *more* for your song than you do. They understand it on a different level.

The ultimate payoff is driving in your car, turning on the radio, and hearing your song. Who gets the biggest thrill out of this: You the writer? Or the publisher? I think it's a toss-up. Your good publisher deserves to work your song.

I'm a Staff Writer

Ah, the rarified air in the songwriting world! "I'm a staff writer" for Big Deal Cool Music Publishing. This situation has its good and bad points.

Staff writer—what does the term mean? A staff writer is a person who has an exclusive contract with a publishing company stating that all the songs the writer creates over the next year, or the term of the contract, belong to the publishing company for the full term of the copyright. That means the company owns the publishing rights. You retain the writer's rights. The publisher may have you include a certain number of songs you have already created. The publisher will expect to receive anywhere from 10 to 50 songs per year from the writer.

Here are the pros and cons: All the money they are paying you is an "advance" against any future earnings. The music publisher is betting that they will not only recoup the bucks expended to pay you a salary, but also make more big bucks beyond what they have paid you. All of the advanced monies will be deducted from future earnings on that copyright. This is legitimate on the publisher's part and is indeed the norm in the music business.

Any monies the publisher has spent on demos will be charged back to you, the writer. This can add up to substantial dollars. So, it is wise on your part to keep a record of the demo dates, the studio, the players, how long you were in the studio, and who the engineer was. How long did the mixes take? This way you will have some idea of what the true cost was of the demo of your song.

For instance, if you recorded three of your songs and there were three of that other writer's songs on the session, you don't want the other writer's part of the session charged back to you. In addition, you should break it down to just your songs that have been recorded.

The good part is that you are getting a livable income and you have access to a demo studio for your use (when the publisher wants a new demo of a song you wrote). Your responsibilities are to write and do your demos for the publisher; he or she then runs around trying to get your songs recorded. The publisher has more incentive to work your songs to justify the expense of paying you.

The focus of this book is all about getting your songs recorded and placed, and getting them listened to so they have a chance. You do not want to lose sight of the fact that you, the songwriter, still have an obligation *to yourself.* This is your career, not the music publisher's career (although they are linked by contract).

Contracts are one thing, but the personal relationship you build with the publisher is very important. You may not always agree with him or her. That's life. You do want to maintain a positive and open creative relationship with him. If, however, she is losing faith in you and your songs, it might be an uphill battle. This is when you take steps and have a meeting about what is not happening on both sides. Publishers are conservative with money and about where they will direct next year's budget, and they are always looking for new talent. If they lose faith in your ability to get recorded (that is, to make them money), it's their option to drop you as a staff writer.

Keep up your contacts and pitch your songs whenever you have the opportunity. Don't sit back and rely on the Big Deal Cool Music publisher.

HOT TIP

> ▸ Honor your commitment to the publisher and give them the best songs you have.

> ▸ The songs are the tools the publisher needs to get a recording.

> ▸ Do not shortchange yourself.

In the history of staff writers, there are many examples of happy careers and partnerships that have lasted for years. By the same token, there are just as many that end in conflict. A common theme is that the writer is let down by the publisher, or at least in the writer's mind. At times, that's exactly it. The music publisher can't get a song recorded. The writer is not living up to the quality of songs the publisher expects. The writer doesn't respond to assignments for a specific artist. The writer is slow in developing material. These, and many other problems, arise.

Sometimes, one of the problems may be personal. As the weeks roll by, the writer and publisher just don't get along. If the individual who signed the writer moves on to another firm, the writer's champion is gone. And since there is no one to champion the writer, the writer feels he or she is now in limbo. Often, this will be the case. What to do? *It is your career*—pitch your songs the best you can. Meet with the publishing staff that is left or with the new person and try to make a connection. Do not give up, and keep a professional attitude.

Here is an example of a nonproducing writer: I once signed someone to write exclusively for my company for a one-year period. This was based on about eight or ten songs the writer played for me, and these songs were included in the deal. As time passed, I didn't receive any more songs from the writer. The writer was waiting for me to get one of the eight songs recorded before he would furnish me with any more material. Stupid! This writer had a reversion clause stating that if any of the songs had not been recorded, all the publishing rights came back in full to the writer after the year!

I signed the writer, hoping to get a number of songs to "work," so as time went on I would have fresh material. About six months into the contract, human nature took over and what had been a great relationship plunged into a very strange ordeal. About nine months into the one-year contract, I stopped pitching this writer's songs. What was the point?

This situation had never happened to me before, or since. Who was hurt? The writer was. I had other writers and songs to work and did so. I got many of those songs recorded. The reluctant writer lost a whole year of a career. Not smart. *It was his career!* A few years later, I met with the writer again and we chalked it up as a misunderstanding of how the business works. Remember: this is a business, not a hobby.

HOT TIP

Remember, you're not dealing with a publishing company or a record company:

▸ You're dealing with a person.

▸ If that person leaves the company, you may not have a deal any longer. On paper you will, but in reality you won't.

▸ Meet with the existing publishing staff or with the new person and try to make a connection.

▸ Do not give up, and keep a professional attitude.

Being a staff writer will introduce you to people in the business whom you may not have been able to meet before. Being a signed writer, or a staff writer, has a certain prestige, a privileged place, a kind of recognition of a better talent. That is not always true, of course, but that's the perception.

If you find yourself in the position as staff writer, work it as smart and as hard as you can. Co-write with other writers. It can be your big ticket as a writer. It is your career. This position can and will open doors for you. Keep creating. Above all, be professional.

Being Your Own Music Publisher

Here are some short tips, with the pros and cons, on being your own music publisher. Being a songwriter is a full-time job. Being a real music publisher is more than a full-time job.

I believe that both are special talents. You as a writer should have more than just a basic grasp of what a publisher does and even how publishing works on an international level. There are many fine books about music publishers, producers, writers, artists, and managers. (See the Appendices for lists of books on music publishing.)

You should, however, know that you own and control your publishing rights from the moment you write your song. Only *you* can give up or sign the publishing rights to a music publisher. Even when you sign the publishing away, you retain the writer's portion.

The publisher's job does not stop when the song is placed, recorded, and released. That's when the publisher must track and collect for the copyright worldwide. Time for the income—finally!

Just so you know, you can be your own publisher. There are plenty of administration companies that, for a percentage fee, handle all the paperwork, licensing, and other duties of a publisher. Many of these companies do an excellent job. Having at least a basic understanding of what they are doing will be a big help to you and your relationship with them.

Final Thoughts

The career of the artist who records your song rides on your shoulders. It is your song that can mean $1 million a year for the artist or $50 million, or only a hundred bucks. Regardless of what you think of the songs the artist records, this is the bottom line.

I believe more real information is packed into this book than any other book you can read about how to get your songs placed and heard. By following the steps laid out for you, your song will be heard by the right people—the decision makers. That's what you want and about all you can ask for. "I listened to your songs, and we're recording next Friday."

HOT TIP

▸ No matter the medium, you still have to get your song in front of those who make decisions, those who decide what song will be used.

▸ Let's make sure it is your song that gets recorded.

▸ It is your career.

▸ Treat it like one.

Appendices

DUDE'S FLOW CHART ... "NOTHING HAPPENS WITHOUT THE SONG"

Career

Establish yourself as the writer who can deliver. You are a hit songwriter; you have a career.

Enjoy

Collect monies from all over the world. Attend Awards. BMI, ASCAP, SESAC, record company. Keep making contacts..

↑

↑

Subpublishing deals

Exploitation of self as hit songwriter

↑

Subpublishing deals

↑

Exploitation

↑

Music publishing company receives 100% of mechanical income.

↑

Platinum

Hit Song by Hit Songwriter/ Big Deal Artist

Gold

Work begins for more songs: keep pitching

Big check comes in the mail. Handle your money close to the vest. Paydays can be few and far between, even for hit writers

While the song is hot; pitch other songs by using the name of your song to help get in the door (step-by-step)

↑

The recording is sold and generates airplay in other countries. (This is a major source of income.)

While the song is hot, pitch to other artists (Keep exploiting the copyright. Pitch for movies, TV, commercials, special projects.)

Album and video sales generate mechanical income (Units sold)

Song is released for airplay (Airplay money is dispersed)

Artist covers the song

Keep Pitching the song

Paid To Publisher ASCAP/BMI/SESAC

Follow through

Follow the guidelines

The "Pitch"

Making contact

Look for old and new avenues for your songs. Think about audits of record labels, and publishers/subpublishers after 3 years of big seller.

Hang gold records. Co-write. Keep creating. Read this book again. Always conduct yourself with dignity.

Career

↑

Enjoy

↑

Keep making new contacts: don't sit back!

↓

Subpublishing deals

↓

Exploitation

↓

Songwriter receives 50% of mechanical income from music publisher

↓

Paid to artist ASCAP/BMI/SESAC

The "Pitch"

Artist	Pitch ▼	Contacts	Demo	Pitch ▲	The "Pitch"
Producer	▼ Pitch		Pitch ▲	Manager	A&R

SONGWRITER

Recommended Organizations

You can find lists for songwriter, music business, and performing rights organizations throughout the world on the Web. Pick your area.

Academy of Country Music

American Society of Composers, Authors, and Publishers (ASCAP)

Association of Independent Music Publishers (AIMP)

Broadcast Music Incorporated (BMI)

California Copyright Conference (CCC)

Canadian Recording Industry Association (CRIA)

Country Music Association (CMA)

Grammy Organization

Harry Fox Agency (for-profit branch of the NMPA)

Just Plain Folks

Nashville Songwriters Association International (NSAI)

National Association of Recording Merchandisers (NARM)

National Music Publishers Association (NMPA)

Recording Industry Association of America (RIAA)

SESAC

SOCAN (Canada)

SongNet Songwriters Guild of America (SGA)

SoundExchange

TAXI

West Coast Songwriters Association

Recommended Reading

Baker, Bob. *MySpace Music Marketing*. St. Louis: Bob Baker Books, 2006.

Baker, Bob. *Online Music PR Directory: 149 Places to Submit Press Releases, Get Reviewed, Uncover PR Connections, and Promote Your Music on the Internet*. St. Louis: Bob Baker Books, 2008.

Brabec, Jeffrey, and Brabec, Todd. *Music, Money, and Success: The Insider's Guide to Making Money in the Music Business*. New York: Music Sales Corp., 2004.

Braheny, John. *The Craft and Business of Songwriting*. Cincinnati: Writer's Digest Books, 2011.

Folkman, Jude. *Musician's Atlas 2010*. Milwaukee: Hal Leonard, 2010. (This book was originally published in 2004, and is updated every year.)

Forest, Greg. *Music Business Contract Library*. Milwaukee: Hal Leonard, 2008.

Frederick, Robin. *Shortcuts to Hit Songwriting: 126 Proven Techniques for Writing Songs That Really Sell*. Calabasas: TAXI Music Books, 2008.

Gordon, Steve. *The Future of the Music Business: How to Succeed with the New Digital Technologies*. Milwaukee: Hal Leonard, 2008.

Kimpel, Dan. *Networking Strategies for the New Music Business*, Boston: Artistpro, 2005.

Krasilovsky, M. William, and Shemel, Sidney (with Jonathan Feinstein and John M. Gross). *This Business of Music*. New York: Billboard Books, 2007.

Kusek, Dave, and Leonhard, Gerd. *The Future of Music: Manifesto for the Digital Music Revolution.* Boston: Berklee Press, 2005.

Lathrop, Tad. *This Business of Global Music Marketing: Global Strategies for Maximizing Your Music's Popularity and Profits,* New York: Watson-Guptill, 2007.

Lathrop, Tad. *This Business of Music Marketing and Promotion.* New York: Watson-Guptill, 2003.

Passman, Donald S. *All You Need to Know About the Music Business.* New York: Free Press, 2009.

Pettigrew, Jim Jr. *The Billboard Guide to Music Publicity.* New York: Watson-Guptill, 1989.

Spellman, Peter. *The Musician's Internet—Online Strategies for Success in the Music Industry.* Boston: Berklee Press, 2001.

Spellman, Peter. *The Self-Promoting Musician.* Boston: Berklee Press, 2008.

Waddell, Ray. *This Business of Concert Promotion and Touring: A Practical Guide to Creating, Selling, Organizing, and Staging Concerts.* New York: Watson-Guptill, 2007.

Partial List Of Artists and Companies with Whom Dude McLean Has Worked as Songwriter, Representative, or Administrator

ABBA

Agnetha (from ABBA)

Air Supply

Gerald Albright

Glenn Ballard

Jonnie Barnett

Battlestar Galactica (TV)

Best Little Whorehouse in Texas (film)

Chuckii Booker

John Braheny

Ed Bruce

Cody Bryant

Craig Burbidge

Johnny Cash

Credence Clearwater Revival

Ray Charles

Kerry Chater

Cher

Columbia/TriStar

Dawnbreaker Music

Dirty Dancing (film)

Duke Ellington

England Dan & John Ford Coley

Evita (film)

Exile

FilmTracks

Randy Goodrum

Whitney Houston

Isley Brothers

Chuck Jackson

The Kendalls

Fred Knobloch

Lambert & Potter

Dave Loggins

Tony Lorrich

Loretta Lynn

Barbara Mandrell

Barry Manilow

Jerry Marcelleno

Johnny Mathis

MCA Music

Parker McGee

Maureen McGovern

Stephanie Mills

Oak Ridge Boys

Pamela Phillips Oland

Paul Overstreet

Lionel Ritchie

Riders of the Purple Sage

Leon Russell

Seals & Crofts

Connie Smith

Statler Brothers

Billy Strange

Tanya Tucker

Twisted Sister

Stevie Ray Vaughan

Jennifer Warnes

Andrew Lloyd WebBer

Bob Wyld

ZZ Top

Index

About the Author

Dude McLean was born in Santa Barbara, California, and was raised in Southern California. Before he entered the music business, he was a United States Marine. He has held high-level positions at music-publishing companies including Dawnbreaker, CMI, and MCA Music. He is president of Legendsong Music and his own Goldentouch Music, and has numerous Gold and Platinum albums. In addition to having a career in the music business, Mr. McLean is an expert in outdoor survival skills and a field editor for *Wilderness Way* magazine. He is an in-demand song consultant and a frequently requested guest speaker and panelist for music industry seminars throughout the United States, discussing music publishing, music administration and licensing, and the art, craft, and business of music. He is a member of key music organizations, including NARAS, where he is a voting member for the Grammy Awards. He can be contacted on his Web site at songconsultant.com.